Rob White
SERIES EDITOR

Edward Buscombe, Colin MacCabe and David Meeker
SERIES CONSULTANTS

Cinema is a fragile medium. Many of the great films now exist, if at all, in damaged or incomplete prints. Concerned about the deterioration in the physical state of our film heritage, the National Film and Television Archive, part of the British Film Institute's Collections Department, has compiled a list of 360 key works in the history of the cinema. The long-term goal of the Archive is to build a collection of perfect showprints of these films, which will then be screened regularly at the National Film Theatre in London in a year-round repertory.

BFI Film Classics is a series of books intended to introduce, interpret and honour these 360 films. Critics, scholars, novelists and those distinguished in the arts have been invited to write on a film of their choice, drawn from the Archive's list. The numerous illustrations have been made specially from the Archive's own prints.

With new titles published each year, the BFI Film Classics series is a unique, authoritative and highly readable guide to the masterpieces of world cinema.

The best movie publishing idea of the decade.
Philip French, *The Observer*

A remarkable series which does all kinds of varied and divergent things.
Michael Wood, *Sight and Sound*

Exquisitely dimensioned ... magnificently concentrated examples of freeform critical poetry.
Uncut

Peter Lorre and Fritz Lang rehearse the café scene (Cinémathèque Française)

BFI FILM
CLASSICS

M

. . . .

Anton Kaes

 Publishing

First published in 2000 by the
BRITISH FILM INSTITUTE
21 Stephen Street, London W1P 2LN

Revised edition 2001

The British Film Institute
promotes greater understanding
and appreciation of, and
access to, film and moving image
culture in the UK.

British Library Cataloguing-in-Publication Data
A catalogue record for this book is available from the British Library

ISBN 0–85170–370–4

Series design by
Andrew Barron & Collis Clements Associates

Typeset in Fournier and Franklin Gothic by
D R Bungay Associates, Burghfield, Berks

Printed in Great Britain by The Cromwell Press, Trowbridge, Wiltshire

CONTENTS

. . . .

ACKNOWLEDGMENTS

I am indebted to a number of friends and colleagues who have shared their enthusiasm for Lang's most complex film and helped improve what I wrote about it. I thank Eric Rentschler most of all, but also Edward Dimendberg, Deniz Göktürk, Sara Hall, Peter Kaes, and especially Walter H. Sokel for reading earlier drafts of the text. Any remaining omissions and infelicities are the result of not heeding their advice. I am also deeply grateful to my editor Rob White for having overseen this project with exceptional engagement, intelligence and patience, and to Tom Cabot for his meticulous preparation of the book. Further thanks go to Eric Ames, Stefan Andriopoulos, Bernard Eisenschitz, Tom Gunning, Kristin Kopp, Wolfgang Mühl-Benninghaus, Lutz Musner, Ines Steiner, Cornelia Vismann, Bernd Widdig and Davina Wilner for discussing the film with me. My film students both at Berkeley and Harvard have also been a great source of inspiration. Special thanks go to the Harvard Film Archive for providing me with the 35mm print of *M*, to Richard Rogers of the Film Study Center at Harvard University for facilitating the frame enlargements and to Sabrina Zanella-Foresi, Katie Trainor and Justin Rice for producing them. I finally owe thanks to Julika Kuschke for helping me find treasures at the Filmarchiv/Bundesarchiv Berlin and, as always, to my friends at the Stiftung Deutsche Kinemathek Berlin for their generous help in all archival matters: Hans Helmut Prinzler and Gero Gandert as well as Wolfgang Jacobsen, Peter Latta, Gerrit Thies, Uta Orluc and Werner Sudendorf. I especially appreciate their willingness to let me quote from an unpublished work journal by Fritz Lang.

The title card. The letter as enigma and stigmata

INTRODUCTION

Yes, the images: a shadow cutting across the poster that announces a reward for the child murderer; Peter Lorre's bulging eyes when he discovers the chalk mark on his shoulder; a high-angle shot of a vacant street corner that coldly records the trapped suspect's futile escape attempts; the disembodied hand of the Law that rescues him from the lynch mob. Yes, but also the sounds: the anguished calls for Elsie across silent images of the empty staircase; the neurotic off-screen whistling of a few bars from Grieg's *Peer Gynt*; and, finally, Lorre's voice – so different in accent, pitch, tone, rhythm and cadence from those around him.

Anyone who has seen Fritz Lang's *M* even once will remember these images and sounds. They are etched indelibly in our minds; they circulate as (often ironic) citations in contemporary culture. Who hasn't seen the commercial for MTV where the letters 'TV' have an 'M' slapped on them? Or the poster of *M*, the 1951 *film noir* remake, which adorns an office wall in *The Player*? Or Woody Allen's homage to *M* in *Shadows and Fog*? Umberto Eco once called *Casablanca* a cult film because it is remembered and quoted in parts and fragments. In this sense, *M* has long been a cult film.

In his famous 1961 television interview, 'Le Dinosaur and le Bébé', Jean-Luc Godard asked Lang which of his forty films he thought would last. Without skipping a beat, Lang replied: '*M*'. Godard agreed. No discussion, no other title given. In a 1995 survey of several hundred German film critics and scholars, *M* was voted the most important German film of all time. Current movie guides typically describe Lang's film as an 'acclaimed classic' or a 'masterpiece'. Leonard Maltin's *Year 2000 Movie and Video Guide* includes it among the '100 Must-See Films of the 20th Century'.

M was not among Germany's top ten features of 1931. The film received mixed reviews and generated only modest box-office returns. But it did trigger discussions beyond the confines of the movie theatre – more so than other films, as the trade papers proudly remarked. I plan to excavate some of the histories that made *M* an event in 1931. I want to reconstruct the discourses which circulated through the film, energising it and, in turn, being energised by it. The price of *M*'s canonisation as a singular work of art has been its gradual unmooring from its historical base; the film's powerful referentiality has faded from view – in my judgment, wrongly so. Understanding the historical milieu in which the film emerged and lived will allow us to recharge it with the rich social, as well as symbolic, energy it once possessed. To know the questions to which *M*'s emphatic modernism was the answer is already half the battle.

Today's newspapers again abound with stories of serial killers, mass murderers, school shootings, 'lone wolves', stockbrokers running amok and veterans carrying the war into the cities. Are killers naturally born? Or are they made? Recent Hollywood movies – *The Silence of the Lambs*; *Copycat*; *Henry: Portrait of a Serial Killer*; *Summer of Sam* and innumerable others – transform serial murder into mass entertainment. Why this fascination, this obsession with carnage, murder and mayhem? Lang's *M* is implicated in these current questions, but responds to them by suggesting through its very form that something else entirely might be negotiated in these films – something that has to do with us, with our lives, our communities, our culture.

. . . .

M has been an unstable text. There is a French version of 1932, *M le Maudit*, for instance, which ends with children dancing in a circle, celebrating, it seems, the capture of the child murderer. (The happy-ending footage was added by the French distributor.) Neglected for many decades, Lang's original *M* of 1931 was re-released in 1959 by Seymour Nebenzal, the original producer, in a heavily altered form: it eliminated references to the powerlessness of the state and its judicial system; it cut out scenes that were not necessary to the narrative; and it added natural sound (such as traffic noise and footsteps) for greater realism. The 1959 version also changed the title to *M. Dein Mörder sieht dich an* (M – Your Murderer Looks at You). When it was shown on German television, the title was altered again to *M. Eine Stadt sucht einen Mörder* (M – A City Searches for a Murderer).

Between 1975 and 1991, Enno Patalas of the Munich Film Museum worked on the restoration of the film. In 1995–96, Donat Keusch refurbished and digitised the original soundtrack. The result of their efforts is now commercially available (also with English subtitles) on film, video, laserdisc and DVD. This restored version, 111 minutes long, comes as close as presently possible to the original film of 1931, which ran a total of 117 minutes. From the 1931 censorship records, which required a transcription of the film's spoken text, we know that one entire scene is missing (published here as an appendix), as are some small portions of the dialogue. We do not know, however, whether Lang himself made these cuts after the premiere. Until 1997, the Anglo-American film and video versions of *M* were based on the shortened version of 1959, which ran for only 89 minutes and was additionally marred by murky sound and inadequate subtitles. Needless to say, my reading follows the restored version.

1
....
BERLIN, 1931

A thundering gong rings out and reverberates over a dark screen for a full ten seconds. Lang, the consummate modernist, begins his film with the medium's bare essentials: a black canvas and a single, resonating sound. This sparseness of means introduces a highly controlled, richly self-reflexive and fully artificial universe in which nothing is left to chance except death. Although set in Berlin, Weimar Germany's bustling metropolis of more than four million people, *M* is entirely a studio production. A contradiction, a paradox? Lang called his film a documentary,[1] and it is one inasmuch as it faithfully records those deep structures of order and disorder which constitute a society in crisis. *M*, as contemporary critics noted, was pulp fiction dealing with serial murder and organised crime, but it is also a parable in the tradition of Franz Kafka: abstract, philosophical and open to endless readings.

Contemporary radio employed gongs to announce the beginning of a program and to mark the precise hour. Lang's unconventional use of this aural cue alerted the spectator from the start to the importance of sound and time. *M* shows a city in a race against time to apprehend a serial killer before he strikes again. Close-ups of clocks and timepieces punctuate the film. Waiting is presented as a test of nerves. A pickpocket, while impatiently expecting the arrival of the crime syndicate's leader, makes a phone call to get the exact time from the operator. He then pulls out seven stolen pocket watches, lines them up in a row, examining and adjusting the time on each. To possess the precise time meant to be in sync with the city, to be a fully functioning component in an unstoppable clockwork. But what if one part malfunctioned, if it followed a different schedule, if it didn't fit and even imperiled the efficiency and rationality of the whole?

A girl's voice can be heard over the black screen, faintly at first, reciting a contemporary nursery rhyme that evoked the gruesome murders of Weimar Germany's most infamous serial killer, Fritz Haarmann, who was caught and executed in 1924. Although the film substitutes his name with 'The Man in Black', it was recognised at the time as the 'Haarmann song'.

> Wait, wait just a little while
> The Man in Black will soon also come to you[2]

The first line of the song, notably preoccupied with time, issues from the dark. We hear a voice, but see no speaker – an 'acousmatic' scene in the words of Michel Chion, who uses this term for sound that is heard without its source being seen.[3] The effect is uncanny; it suggests some higher command directed at the viewer: wait and the man in black will soon also come to *you*.

Lang was fascinated with the new opportunities that sound afforded for redefining the relationship between screen and audience. In his unpublished work journal of 1930–31 (only recently discovered), he jotted down notes about innovative uses of sound in *M*:

> Shouldn't one radically break the frame of a sound film by directly addressing the audience, by turning to them with the help of loudspeakers? Be it as a moralist, as a chronicler, as a commentator . . . Address by the loudspeaker, by the poet to the audience. Begin with 'Watch out and listen! Crimes have been committed, so horrifying, so terrible, so inhuman, etc.'[4]

Lang wanted sound to be independent from the movie itself so that it might mediate between the film and the audience, just as in early film a lecturer stood next to the screen and explained the movie's action to the audience. Sound which had already expanded the visual dimension laterally into off-screen space was now to extend outwards and speak directly, free of all diegetic constraints, to the viewers. Erwin Piscator and Bertolt Brecht had experimented with similar appeals to the audience. For them, foregrounding the apparatus was the first step in their ideological critique of classical bourgeois theatre that saw itself as separate from 'real life'. For Lang, however, the loudspeaker effect was less an instrument of political agitation than a form of audience control. Although, in the end, Lang did not put this idea into practice, the journal entry reveals his desire to rethink the entire filmic apparatus in the wake of the sound revolution.

As the girl's voice grows louder, the image opens to an overhead shot of a circle of children playing a game of 'You're Out'. A girl in the middle points with an extended arm at individual children as she recites each syllable of the rhyme. Turning from child to child, her arm becomes like the hand of a clock, mechanically rotating and suggesting the urgency and inexorability of time. Whoever the hand points to at the last word of the rhyme ('... With his little axe, he'll make mince meat out of *you*') must leave the circle: 'You are out.' Pure chance and fate determine where the finger comes to rest – and where the serial murderer meets his next victim.

While the children's game mimics the nature of serial killing (anyone could be next), the camera's look from above underscores a cold, analytical attitude characteristic of the film in general. No child is singled out through close-up, there is no eye-level position that might support emotional cathexis: the camera simply records the unrelenting process of the serial elimination of one child after another. Rhyme (not reason) decides who will be next as the sound of the girl's voice identifies each new victim.

The scene is set in a Berlin tenement courtyard (*Hinterhof*), surrounded by multi-storeyed buildings and visible, like Bentham's panopticon, from all sides. Although the space seems protected and safe, the murderer's spirit has invaded it through the sound of the gruesome nursery rhyme which, in serial fashion, is repeated three times. It is still heard when the camera begins to pan from the children's circle across the courtyard in order to explore the children's ambience. The camera's movement is jerky, as if hand-held, thus calling attention to itself. As the camera slowly moves upwards, it captures in passing two garbage bins. A chain of associations begins to form that links naïve children, murder and refuse – a first map of reference points that will be elaborated in the following scenes. The camera comes to rest at a railing which cuts across the image, presenting a picture of division and separation, a tension between above, where the mothers work, and below, where the children play. The children's song off-screen, with its allusions to elimination and deprivation, underlies and intensifies the desolate images. Lang's off-screen sound expands the field of vision and suggests a space outside the frame, but it also provides a commentary on what the camera shows.

Cut to an empty staircase. A pregnant woman with a heavy basket of laundry enters the frame from below. The all-knowing camera awaits her. Through its very movement, angle, distance and length of take, the camera comments, investigates and exposes. And, like the narrator in a

A morbid game

'You're out'

A far off mother

novel by Balzac, it pretends to be omniscient, assuming, as D. A. Miller put it, 'a fully panoptic view of the world it places under surveillance. Nothing worth knowing escapes its notation and its complete knowledge includes the knowledge it is always right.'[5]

In *M*'s first scene, the camera separates the mothers (there are no men in sight) from their children by walls, balconies, railings and closed doors. After the washerwoman has climbed the stairs, she shouts down to the children to stop chanting that 'awful song', aware more than the children of the song's power to conjure up the mass murderer's appearance. As in 1931 Berlin, aggression, gloom and apprehension are palpable. The mother's interdiction stops the song for only a few seconds; the children (outside the frame) quickly resume the nursery rhyme. The result is at once funny and foreboding; the children do what they like, openly disobeying the mother's command, challenging her weak authority. They continue their game that playfully enacts serial elimination. Mrs Beckmann puts a positive spin on their wilful misconduct, emphasising the importance of sound: 'As long as they're singing, at least we know they're still there.'

Sound affirms presence and life; silence connotes absence and death. When Elsie is murdered and Mrs Beckmann's anguished calls for her across an empty staircase and attic cease, the sound film falls silent. The moving picture freezes on Elsie's empty chair (shot from above in the stark style of Bauhaus photography), on her clean plate, her spoon, her cup and her folded napkin, all neatly (and now pointlessly) laid out on the kitchen table. Inanimate objects stand in for an absent – and violently silenced – person. Coming after the cries, the silence is eerie. We have no doubt about Elsie's

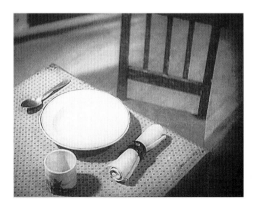

Signs of absence

fate. Cut to a dry area of shrubs. Elsie's ball slowly rolls into the frame and comes to an unsteady halt, at once evoking her (because it was her toy) and metonymically replacing her. This haunting shot is followed by Elsie's huge balloon with its painted face and miniature arms, animistically come

The anthropomorphic balloon

alive in its resemblance to her. After becoming entangled in the telegraph wires for a few seconds, it weightlessly drifts skywards.

Once again, the screen darkens for several seconds and opens to a sound collage of newspaper vendors running down the streets shouting: 'Extraausgabe, Extraausgabe!' ('Extra, extra, read all about it!'). Within no time, Elsie's murder has become a headline story. The transition from the sight of telegraph wires, touched and activated, as it were, by Elsie's abandoned balloon, to the sound of street hawkers essentialises the unprecedented speed with which information was disseminated in 1931 Berlin. At their crescendo, the sounds take on a threatening quality, suggesting the increasingly irrational pursuit of more and faster sensations.

. . . .

The making of *M* coincided with the rapid disintegration of the political and social structures of the Weimar Republic. In June 1930, when the first notices about Fritz Lang's new, still untitled film project were published in *Film-Kurier*,[6] the worldwide recession had reached Germany in the form of massive unemployment, rising criminality and political unrest. In September 1930, millions of disenfranchised and embittered workers voted for the National Socialists, catapulting the number of seats held by the Nazi party from 12 to 107, and making it the second-largest group in the German parliament. When Lang was shooting *M* in the Staaken studios (a former Zeppelin hangar from World War I) outside Berlin from mid-January to February 1931, Germany's capital became the site of wild strikes, mass demonstrations and street battles. *M*, the original title of which was *Mörder unter uns* (meaning either Murderers or Murderer among Us), captures the irritable and explosive atmosphere of Germany two years before Hitler's assumption of power. At a time of widespread political violence, a title such as *Murderers among Us* could easily be misunderstood. Lynch mobs and hit commandos engaged in open manhunts, intimidating political enemies and spreading terror among the population. The newspapers were filled with daily reports of violent, often deadly clashes and attacks. A contemporary, well-publicised court case against members of the SA (Sturmabteilung or Storm Troops, a.k.a. Brown Shirts), shadowed the production of *M* and culminated in a murder trial which carried echoes of the film's own mock trial.

In the late fall of 1930, hit men of the SA, Hitler's private army, had targeted, chased and killed a member of the Communist party. The highlight of the six-week trial was Hitler's appearance as a witness, three days before *M* opened. When he entered the courtroom, the defendants jumped up to greet him with 'Heil Hitler.' The judge was not amused. Boisterous young SA members filled the hall and accompanied the proceedings with applause or whistles. Hitler was asked whether the SA commando had planned the murder, 'with the purpose to kill people intentionally and with predetermination and whether these deeds are known to the party leadership and condoned by it'.[7] In other words, were the Nazis 'murderers among us'?

By 1931, the SA had become a major underground political force of more than 100,000 men who controlled the streets and attacked anyone thought to be an enemy of the Nazi doctrine. They kept Berlin (and other cities in Germany) in a state of permanent alarm and nervous agitation. Hitler was aware of their dubious legal status (they were occasionally banned) and had to keep them from independent revolutionary action, particularly after Ernst Roehm assumed leadership in January 1931. Political murders were common; the punishment, if a crime came to trial at all, was minimal. In this court case, Hitler denied any knowledge of party-sanctioned murder: 'The National Socialist party has never given the order: Strike the enemy dead. Strike the Communists dead. Strike the

Social Democrats dead.' He went on to say that he condemned bombs, guns and violence. 'I would be for these methods only if a single person suppressed the German people. But our misfortune does not lie in the guilt of individual persons ... it lies in a certain mind-set in which our people find themselves.' Hitler portrayed himself as a victim and claimed that his appeals for restraint provoked others to call him 'cowardly, bourgeois, complacent and small-minded'. A week after *M* opened, the court case ended with mild jail sentences for the murderers.

Whether Lang saw his film as a possible intervention in the precarious political situation of 1930–31 remains unclear. He later claimed that the original title *Murderers among Us* had caused him numerous problems: the Nazis thought the title referred to them. No evidence supports this claim beyond Lang's oft-told anecdote of how he grabbed the hostile studio manager by the lapel and noticed a swastika pin behind it. An official reason for the title change, however, can be found in the *Film-Kurier* of 20 April 1931: 'The original title, *Murderers among Us*, cannot be used because of several other films with the word "murderer" in their titles; therefore the new film title will come from a sign which plays a role in the film itself.'[8] From *Murderers among Us* to *M*: the title change (only three weeks before the premiere) may have determined the life of the movie. Titles raise expectations and prestructure responses. *Murderers among Us* promises sensationalist and melodramatic pulp fiction. *M*, by contrast, is abstract, spare and ambiguous, an enigma and an incentive for speculation. No question, this mysterious title stood out among the 144 other German feature films produced in 1931.

. . . .

Lang wanted his new film to stand out: *M* marked his return to the film scene after a nineteen-month absence. Rumours had spread about his fundamental opposition to sound. Lang's last silent film, *Die Frau im Mond* (Woman in the Moon), which opened on 15 October 1929, had not been a happy experience. It appeared in the middle of the sound revolution and looked strangely old-fashioned, even though it featured, as is usual in a sci-fi film, various sorts of technological inventions, including a rocket to the moon. When the Universum Film AG (Ufa) urged Lang to 'modernise' the film and add a soundtrack, he flatly refused and instead left his long-term employer before his contract expired. (Hitchcock, by contrast, did not hesitate in 1929 to add sound to *Blackmail*, which he had shot as a silent film.)

Was Germany's most ambitious director out of touch with current trends? All of Lang's silent films – particularly *Der müde Tod* (Destiny, 1921), the two-part *Dr. Mabuse* (1922), as well as the two-part *Nibelungen* (1924) and the 3½-hour *Metropolis* (1926–27) – had been critical and even, in part, commercial triumphs; they were also internationally acclaimed and celebrated. But his latest two films, *Spione* (Spies, 1928) and *Woman in the Moon* had fared less well. A fresh start was needed. While the story of *Woman in the Moon* was freely invented and convoluted, mixing high-tech sci-fi and maudlin melodrama, the story of *M* addressed events of the time and disallowed identification or emotional cathexis. At once a documentary of Berlin's underworld and a modernist art film, it oscillated between detailed reportage and abstract ornament. It featured no attractive, new young actress, no romantic interest. There was as little love lost in the film as there was between Lang and his wife Thea von Harbou. After his open but brief and ill-fated affair with Gerda Maurus (who played the lead in *Woman in the Moon*), Lang and Harbou separated, although their decade-long collaboration continued. Because the screenplay is lost, we do not know how much was added or changed between the completion of the script in May 1930 and the actual production which began in January 1931. The film's credits list Thea von Harbou as the sole author of the screenplay.

Did *M* mark a return to *Dr. Mabuse* and the crime film tradition of the early 1920s, as some critics surmised? *Dr. Mabuse*, of course, was a silent film, featuring a Nietzschean supercriminal who uses his hypnotic gaze to manipulate the stockmarket and to wreak havoc among the

Adolf Jansen, Fritz Lang, Thea von Harbou, Fritz Arno Wagner (Cinémathèque Française)

decadent upper class. How different from *M*! Sound alone demoted the criminal; he now was a subject tormented by his own uncontrollable whistling and spooked by the sounds of his pursuers. If Mabuse imposed his will through the power of the look, the child murderer in *M*, more the object than the bearer of the gaze, is eventually betrayed by sound. For Lang, it was not a matter of adding a soundtrack to a silent film, but one of making the new technology a structural feature of the narrative itself. Sound became a signifying code that radically reconfigured the nature of the image, of vision, of film in general.

Lang was the last major German film director to adopt sound. The German film industry itself had been slow to make the costly transition, which could not have come at a worse time in the industry's history. The economic crisis after 1929 had reduced movie attendance by almost a third (from 328 million to 238 million between 1929 and 1932) and had drastically cut back the number of feature films made in Germany, from 183 in 1929 to 144 in 1931. Theatre owners hesitated to purchase and install expensive new sound projectors, while production companies did not want to make sound films that could not be shown. Reports of the commercial success of American sound films and the attendant fear of being left behind in the international market finally shocked the German film industry into action.

In a concerted attempt to modernise, Ufa built in record time four state-of-the-art sound studios in Neubabelsberg in the summer of 1929. They were used for Josef von Sternberg's *The Blue Angel*, one of Ufa's first major sound films, which opened with great fanfare on 1 April 1930. Sound was here to stay: by the autumn of 1930 every film was a sound film. It may have been due to the rapidly spreading use of radio in the late 1920s that the emergence and full acceptance of the sound film was made possible and even inevitable. As radio technology improved, the number of subscribers grew exponentially: from 200 in 1923 to 100,000 in 1924, 1 million in 1926, 2 million in 1928 and more than 4 million in 1932. After radio had become 'a household item like potted plants', as O. A. Palitzsch wrote in 1927,[9] it could be assumed that most movie-goers were also radio listeners. They had grown accustomed to disembodied voices, to music that came from a wooden box and to sounds the origins of which often had to be imagined.

Germany, at the height of its silent cinema tradition, resisted the coming of sound more than other countries. Even such progressive critics as Rudolf Arnheim first criticised sound as a throwback to cinema's dependence on theatre and a travesty of all the efforts to develop an autonomous visual language. Lang was unwilling to forsake the formative approach to film-making in which filming meant reconstituting, not recording, reality. As late as January 1929, when discussions of sound cinema filled the air, Fritz Lang extolled the virtues of the silent film in an essay entitled 'The Mimic Art in the Moving Picture'. Following Béla Balázs's theory of silent cinema from his 1924 book, *The Visible Man*, Lang argued that the close-up in silent film allowed viewers to read gestures and facial and body movements as means of unlocking a character's inner secrets and rediscovering the human face in all its expressiveness. 'Before film did we know how much could be signified by a closed mouth twitching, an eyelid rising and falling, a head quietly turning away?'[10] Early film had made movie-goers into experts in physiognomy – a genuine achievement of silent cinema in Lang's view. Asked by the *Film-Kurier* on 1 July 1930 whether he would consider making another silent film, Lang's answer was an emphatic 'no'. But so far, he added, sound had done nothing to enhance the artistic potential of cinema. In his next film, he wanted to find ways to create a sound film 'that can carry on the heritage of silent film'.[11] Lang's *M* has rightly been called a 'silent film with sound'.[12] It is a transitional film in its sparing and expressive use of sound, squarely in the tradition of Dreyer's *Vampyr* (1932), Vertov's *Enthusiasm* (1930), Buñuel's *L'Âge d'or* (1930) and Clair's *À nous la liberté* (1931). This 'heritage of silent film' in sound referred to the self-expressiveness of voices and noises – a tradition that originated from radio and telephone, where pitch and volume, inflection and intonation, rhythm and cadence compensated for the bodily absence of persons and things.

. . . .

M's complex sound collages are closer to Walther Ruttmann's acoustic film experiment *Weekend* (1930) than to the contemporary musicals and operettas produced by Ufa to flaunt the new invention.[13] Ruttmann's *Weekend* was a remarkable hybrid between film and radio, consisting of an elaborate composition of voices and noises, clamour and music, all rhythmically arranged to evoke images of weekend activities. It was an eleven-minute film of sound without images, presented in May 1930 as a radio play in a film theatre before a closed curtain. Paul Falkenberg, Lang's sound editor and a close friend of Ruttmann's, drew inspiration from *Weekend* for *M*'s richly cadenced sound collages (for example, noontime is evoked by the sounds of clocks, chimes and bells); the use of crescendo (people's voices rising to a din); and the conscious employment of signature sounds (the obsessive whistle; the noisy honking of car horns; the insistent tapping of a nail). These noises do not simply accompany the images; they carry a strong signifying potential on their own, as if used in a radio play.

Lang's expressionist heritage, in particular its acknowledgment of the psyche's power to subjectivise and thus 'distort' the visible world, was to be extended to sound. When, for instance, the blind balloon seller covers his ears to stifle the noise of a cacophonous hurdy-gurdy, the diegetic sound suddenly stops; he lifts his hands and the sound is heard again. We hear only what he hears. This approximates what could be called an acoustic point-of-view. What looks here like a mere stylistic exercise to foreground the subjective perception of sound sensitises us to read a later scene in which the child murderer is *not* able to control the sound spinning in his head. Visibly agitated, he sits in an outdoor café and drinks brandy. As he stares in front of him, the *Peer Gynt* melody suddenly starts up again; it is unclear from where it emanates. The sound must be subjective, imagined, hallucinated because now the whistling continues, mercilessly, even after he covers both ears. Unlike the balloon seller, Beckert has no power over what he hears. The whistling is a marker of his unconscious self, a dramatic sign that in its repeated recurrence 'gives wordless expression to his inner urges'.[14] Like a Wagnerian leitmotif, the whistle follows Beckert as a preverbal articulation and external symptom of his compulsions. It pathologises him from the beginning.

Lang uses sound not only for dialogue and communication. *M*'s sound collages often express the unconscious of a character or the unspoken implications of a scene. Likewise, the whistling reveals precisely what cannot be put into words. When we first see Inspector Lohmann, we note that he also whistles. Thus the film's sound subtly establishes hidden cross-references and unacknowledged affinities between Lohmann and Beckert – both are single and physically unappealing, both are compulsive players in a hide-and-seek game. Beckert's whistling, which seems to come from off-screen (it is in fact Lang's own whistling because Lorre could not whistle), also betrays a split between sound and body. He is identified at the precise moment the blind beggar connects a sound to a body.

The tune, drawn from Edvard Grieg's *Peer Gynt* ('In the Hall of the Mountain King'), refers to a terrifying scene in the eponymous Ibsen play where the trolls attack the trespassing Peer Gynt with repeated screams of 'Slaughter him, slaughter him, tear him up, tear him up.' *Peer Gynt* was staged in Berlin in 1928, in a famous production by Berthold Viertel (with Werner Krauß, well-known from his role as Dr Caligari) that Lang had almost certainly seen. *M*'s frenzied mob, yelling and shrieking like the trolls, enacts the command that Beckert's own whistling of the *Peer Gynt* tune had evoked all along. The sound subtly exteriorises his subconscious, also suggesting the punishment that he expects and wants. The whistling implies an involuntary self-surveillance.

When Lang embarked on his first sound film, it was important that he have a producer with a knowledge of the new technology. After his rancorous separation from Ufa in spring 1930, he signed a contract with the small independent production company Nero-Film, the energetic young owner of which, Seymour Nebenzahl, granted Lang complete artistic freedom. Responsible for some of the finest silent films of 1929 – G. W. Pabst's *Die Büchse der Pandora* (Pandora's Box) and the experimental semi-documentary film *Menschen am Sonntag* (People on Sunday) with Robert and Curt Siodmak, Edgard G. Ulmer and Billy Wilder – Nero-Film also produced Pabst's significant early sound features *Westfront 1918* (1930) and *Die 3-Groschen-Oper* (The Threepenny Opera), the controversial film adaptation of Brecht's musical play, which premiered on 19 February 1931. The latter led to a much-publicised lawsuit between Brecht and Nero-Film over the status of the author in the film industry. The company, small in comparison to the Ufa conglomerate, but independent and with a leftist image, was a financially secure and serious alternative to Ufa. Still, money was tight and the short shooting time of six weeks (very unusual for Lang) was to save money. So was the practice, as described by the *Film-Kurier*, of shooting two-thirds of the film without sound to avoid paying license fees for the use of Tobis Klangfilm equipment. Lang hired one of the most brilliant and experienced cameramen of the 1920s, Fritz Arno Wagner, whose work ranged from F. W. Murnau's expressionism to G. W. Pabst's New Objectivity realism. According to the trade papers which regularly reported on the film's progress, Lang and Falkenberg, his sound editor, collaborated in the editing of the film during March 1931. (Early sound cinema employed special editors who recorded the sounds separately from the images in order to finesse and 'edit' the soundtrack, working with scissors to produce collage effects. Image and sound became joined on one strip only at the very end.) *M* was submitted to the Berlin Censorship Board on 27 April 1931 and – to everyone's surprise – passed without a cut.

. . . .

When *M* opened on 11 May 1931 at the largest and most prestigious film theatre in Berlin, the Ufa-Palast am Zoo, luminaries from the political, financial and cultural world were in attendance. Outside the theatre, an unruly mob clashed with the police, unwittingly reproducing scenes from the movie playing inside. Slightly amused by this confluence of art and life, the reporter for the *Film-Kurie*r (12 May 1931) wondered whether reality might have taken its cue from Lang's new film.

What struck most critics first was *M*'s topicality. Place and time were current – Berlin in the fall of 1930, with several newspapers showing clearly readable titles and dates – as was the film's story about an elusive serial killer. *M* presents a society at war with itself. Serial murder recalled wartime slaughter, and the heightened state of mobilisation of an entire community echoed experiences from the home front. War films, increasingly popular at the end of the 1920s, reminded audiences of the trauma of mass death and collective hysteria, thus providing a receptive climate for *M*. The film's focus on the downtrodden lumpenproletariat, on washerwomen and fatherless children, criminals and beggars, haggard prostitutes and slovenly policemen, dramatised the widespread unemployment and economic misery in the wake of the 1929 stockmarket crash. Life in the last few years of the Weimar Republic was in a permanent state of crisis.

The chasm between cultural and political life, always an issue in the Weimar Republic, was never wider than in 1931. While the majority of the public drifted to the reactionary right, most of the cultural production was unabashedly leftist, critical, innovative and more vibrant than ever. The social turmoil injected a sense of urgency and mission. Theatre, traditionally Germany's most vaunted art form, took up the challenge, responding to the most pressing social issues in the period between 1928 and 1932. The so-called *Zeittheater* (theatre of current events) openly dealt with such problems as abortion (F. Wolf's *Cyankali*), criminality (F. Bruckner, *Die Verbrecher*/The Criminals), rebellious youth (P. M. Lampel, *Revolte im Erziehungsheim* / Revolt in the Reform School), sexuality (Fleisser, *Pioniere in Ingolstadt* / Pioneers in Ingolstadt) and the war experience (G. Weisenborn, *U-Boot S 4*). As a late outgrowth of New Objectivity, the dominant art movement in the mid-1920s, the *Zeittheater* strove to deal with burning social issues in a documentary and authentic manner. Although Lang shared with the *Zeittheater* an interest in sociological questions, his work probed more deeply, especially in his concern with the psychopathology of the criminal mind. Nevertheless, in 1931, *M* was often referred to as a '*Zeitfilm*'. Discussions particularly concentrated on the spirited arguments made for and against the death penalty; the treatment of mentally ill criminals; and the safety of children.

Weimar's rich cultural milieu is especially evident in the film's astonishing casting, which made full use of Berlin's distinguished theatrical elite. Despite the recession in 1930–31, Berlin's theatre still offered some of the most original and provocative productions, with the best acting talent in Europe. Germany's media capital attracted stage actors who also worked in radio and film. Gustaf Gründgens, who plays Schränker, the arrogant leader of the criminal underworld, was the most prominent of the actors who moved effortlessly between stage and screen. He began his film career after 1929 when sound film needed players with perfect diction. His famous role as Robespierre in *Danton* (only a few month prior to *M*), brought out the terrifying coldness that he again displayed in Lang's film. Every actress and actor that Lang engaged (with the exception of little Elsie and some extras from the underworld) had played major roles in the theatre of the 1920s. Several of them were affiliated with Bertolt Brecht, who was at the height of his German renown in 1931. Ellen Widmann (Mrs Beckmann) was well known for her working-class roles, Rosa Valetti (the barkeeper) played in Brecht and Weill's *Dreigroschenoper* (Threepenny Opera), Otto Wernicke (Detective Lohmann) was an established stage actor and the lead in Brecht's *Im Dickicht der Städte* (In the Jungle of Cities); his assistant Theodor Loos (Detective Groeber) had made a name for himself in the proletarian theatre of the 1920s.

It was Brecht who had first discovered Peter Lorre, a young actor born in 1904 who had come from Hungary to work in Berlin. Lang saw Lorre perform in a Brechtian production of Marieluise Fleisser's episodic play *Pioneers in Ingolstadt* in 1929. Intrigued by Lorre's unusual voice and Austro-Hungarian accent (which may have reminded Lang of his own Viennese background), as well as by the actor's odd looks and self-reflective acting style, Lang wanted him to play the main role in his first sound film. He even made him promise not to accept any other film offers. Lorre initially did not want to give up the stage and continued rehearsals for Brecht's play *Mann ist Mann* (A Man's a Man), staged by the playwright himself to demonstrate his theories of Epic Theatre. Lorre appeared on stage at night, while shooting *M* during the day. Promoted by Brecht as the ideal actor for Epic Theatre, Lorre developed an acting style that was meant to de-psychologise the play: the characters' inner feelings were less important than their social interaction. To shift emphasis from psychology to sociology, from empathy to critical distance, from organic development to montage, from suggestion to argument – this was the project of Brecht's Epic Theatre in 1930 which resonates with Lang's own project. Was he influenced by Brecht? Lang replied in 1963: 'Certainly. Who was not? ... Can one simply ignore a genius like Brecht? Which does not mean one has to embrace his philosophy.'[15] *M* shares with Epic Theatre an episodic structure and an indirect, presentational style. A typical scenario shows a character speaking, while the camera cuts away to vignettes which illustrate (and occasionally undermine) what is said. In the spirit of Epic Theatre this technique turns viewers into private eyes, looking for clues and registering contradictions between word and image.

In Brecht's *A Man's a Man* Lorre played the lead character, Galy Gay, a simpleton who is transformed from a weakling into a war hero when he joins the army. Brecht was interested in the precarious status of the subject in the collective – can a cipher be marked, taken apart and reassembled like a car, as Brecht ironically asserted? Or is the subject, as in *M*, forever trapped in his flawed subjectivity? Lorre's monologue at the end of the film – 'I want to escape ... to escape from myself!' – addressed Brecht's question, but does not provide a solution. Brecht does suggest one, albeit a paradoxical and highly ambivalent one ('forget your identity'), which he soon revised. Is *M* the psychopathological answer to Brecht's provocatively behaviourist *A Man's a Man*? When Brecht's play had its premiere on 6 February 1931 (while *M* was still in production), tumultuous protests from the audience interrupted the performance. Pictures show Lorre in heavy white make-up and armed to the hilt, while the other soldiers, wearing grotesque face masks, stand on stilts. When the protests, mostly staged by the militant right, continued, the play was cancelled after only five performances.

What did Lang see in Lorre? The theatre critic Kurt Pinthus characterised Lorre's debut in Fleisser's play as follows: 'A new face was there, a horrifying face, the hysterical son of the petty bourgeoisie, whose goggle-eyed, bloated head spilled forth yellowish from his suit. I have hardly ever seen anything as uncanny in theatre as the way this fellow sways between phlegmatism and hysterical outbreak, between a gingerly walk and a greedy touch …'[16] This description anticipates Lorre's appearance in *M* and it almost seems as if Lang and Harbou had written the screenplay with this dramatic persona in mind. Lorre fascinated Lang because his round, child-like face and his corpulent body seemed to conceal a demonic force which might erupt at any moment. Epic acting brought out the contradictions between his destructive (and implicitly self-destructive) impulses and his social roles – he is both the good uncle and the child murderer. Lorre's acting emphasised the split between the person and his deeds, leading the audience to wonder who he 'really' was.

For Lang, Lorre's performance revealed the danger and hysteria lurking behind the indolent bourgeois façade, epitomising what Lang wanted the film as a whole to portray: a society in the grip of self-destructive urges.

When the shooting for Lang and the rehearsals for Brecht conflicted, Lorre decided in favour of his stage work. Lang had to remind him of his contractual obligations, even threatening him with an injunction to appear at the studio. The relationship between Lang and Lorre was reputed to be extremely tense, with Lang playing the same sadistic tricks on him as on all other actors in order to elicit their best performances. This arrogant behaviour may explain why Lorre never again worked with Lang, a fellow emigrant in Hollywood between 1934 and 1964. If

Lorre as a soldier in Brecht's *A Man's a Man* (1931)

M made Lorre a film star, Lorre also made *M* what it is. For many critics then and now, the film's centre of gravity lies in Lorre's unique dramatic persona. In the final analysis, is not *M* as much a Peter Lorre film as it is a Fritz Lang film?

2

SERIAL MURDER, SERIAL CULTURE

The doorbell rings twice. It must be Elsie, late from school. Her mother, Mrs Beckmann, hurries across the kitchen to open the door. But it is Mr Gehrke who delivers the latest instalment of a crime serial. 'New instalment, Mrs Beckmann. Thrilling, stimulating, sensational.' The woman, clearly disappointed, sighs, 'Oh, yes,' and leaves the frame to get a coin. The excitement he brings – lurid tales of crime and passion – stands in ironic contrast to his mechanical voice and dull demeanour. Picking up two more instalments from his satchel, he awkwardly and impatiently waits at the door. Asked if he had seen little Elsie, he replies no. From an earlier scene, we know that well-dressed parents met their children at the school gate, while Elsie's mother works at home. Our first glimpse of Elsie shows her vulnerability: she steps off the sidewalk and is almost run over by a car. Its threatening presence is signaled by a blaring honking noise even before we see it. A policeman accompanies her across the street, unwittingly delivering her to the murderer. While the other children walk with their mothers or fathers, Elsie bounces a ball as she saunters home

Mr Gehrke and Mrs Beckmann

alone. The camera follows her closely in a tracking shot, isolating her from other pedestrians and preparing the viewer for her eventual fate. While Mrs Beckmann prepares lunch for her daughter, Elsie traverses the city unprotected and defenceless. The cross-cutting emphasises the spatial separation between mother and child.

After Mr Gehrke has left, Mrs Beckmann, now visibly agitated, goes to close the door, but hesitates and walks to the staircase, which is shown from her point of view in an extreme high-angle shot. It extends down four storeys, a series of railings and steps in stark symmetry, cold, empty and silent until we hear the mother frantically call out Elsie's name. No answer. She walks the few steps back to her apartment, still holding in her left hand her weekly dose of pulp fiction, lifting it slightly in frustration. And once more, a third time, she looks to the cuckoo clock on the wall. In close-up, it strikes 1:15.

Just before Mr Gehrke delivered the weekly crime serial, we had witnessed a strange encounter: as Elsie bounces her ball against an advertising pillar, the shadow of a head, covering the word 'murderer' on a police poster, appears out of nowhere, bends down and, in a high-pitched voice, addresses the girl. 'My, what a pretty ball you have. What's your name?' The first image of the murderer: a shadow, the phantom-like, immaterial double that points to an unseen body, and a disembodied voice. A sense of unreality and imminent danger pervades the scene. Cut back to the kitchen where Elsie's mother, in a disturbing parallel, bends over (with a knife in her hand, peeling a potato) in the exact same angle as the child murderer's shadow. Cut to the street where

First view of the murderer

Photographing the shadow
(Cinémathèque Française)

we see from high above a man buy Elsie a balloon. After he walks off with the child, the film cuts back to Mrs Beckmann opening the door. The editing suggests that Elsie's murder (the latest in a series of murders) is committed at the precise moment Mrs Beckmann receives the latest instalment of her crime serial. Serial killing and serial fiction echo each other with cruel irony: the crime that is committed already exists in fiction. It is only fitting that we do not see the actual murder. Mr Gehrke's selling of serial murder fiction (and Mrs Beckmann's subscription) implicates Lang's own film as it capitalises on the public's strange fascination with murder and mayhem. It also suggests, none too subtly, a deeper link between representation and action, between mass culture and mass murder. Instead of showing the crime, Lang intimates how imagined murder displaces and, literally, shields us from real murder, which ironically itself will become grist for the media only minutes after the deed. Murder and its mass-marketed representations feed on each other in constant serial repetition.

The viewers of *M* no less than Mrs Beckmann have become unwitting participants in a mass culture that lives off crime. Serial novels turn transgression (real and imagined) into sensationalist fiction; they titillate, arouse and entertain by exploring areas where desire and discipline cross. It is hard to say which appealed more to the downtrodden masses who craved their weekly pulp fiction fix: crime as an attack against a society that has neglected them or the inevitable punishment of those who dared to challenge the law. In either case, serial crime novels provided a vicarious, compensatory experience for those who were discontent with their lives, but unable to change them.

Even more than serial pulp fiction, the daily press had played a major role in disseminating representations of crime. Serial killings were a favourite subject matter at the time of the Weimar Republic; serial crime reinforced the newspaper's own seriality. Peter Kürten, the 'Vampire of Düsseldorf', proudly admitted in court that he had learned from the press about Jack the Ripper, the infamous serial killer in London at the end of the nineteenth century, himself the object of innumerable accounts at the time. (G. W. Pabst's *Pandora's Box*, which opened in February 1929, at the beginning of Kürten's killing spree, featured a romanticised Jack the Ripper.) It was Kürten's desire to become as famous as his British predecessor. 'I can confess now that I had become strongly intoxicated by a sensationalist press which I used to call poison and that the press was also guilty in poisoning my life.'[17] Blaming the murders on the press was probably not original in 1931, but his reasoning did touch on something Lang's film wanted to explore: the price of mass culture's fascination with crime.

In keeping with a general erosion of public trust and governmental authority after the lost war, a failed revolution and a devastating inflation, the Weimar Republic saw violent crime as symptom of a system that seemed rotten at the core. The assassinations of political adversaries in the early 1920s set the stage for subsequent highly publicised murders. Weimar culture was a 'wound culture', where serial killing and serial culture were of one piece.[18] An unprecedented interest in crime and criminology permeated this crisis-ridden society. Respected writers edited a book series, Outsiders of Society, which dealt with famous criminal murder cases; former police commissioners recounted their experiences in books and radio broadcasts; translations of Edgar Wallace became bestsellers; prominent con men published their autobiographies. Convicted putschist Hitler, in his autobiography *Mein Kampf* (written in prison and published in 1925), openly propagated the overthrow of the government. Musical dramas such as *Die Dreigroschenoper* glamorised the criminal underworld. Alfred Döblin's magisterial city novel *Berlin Alexanderplatz* (1929) follows the life of Franz Biberkopf, an ex-convict, in the urban labyrinth of working-class Berlin, a Mecca of petty criminals, prostitutes and pimps. Robert Musil's *Der Mann ohne Eigenschaften* (The Man without Qualities), published first in 1931, featured Moosbrugger, a mass murderer.

A popular daily, *Berliner Morgenpost*, offered in the late 1920s a regular section, called 'Der Kriminalist', in which accounts of real murders appeared side by side with instalments of crime novels. For instance, on 25 November 1929, a long article, entitled 'War in Düsseldorf', described Peter Kürten's latest killing spree; on the same page, opposite this factual (but rhetorically embellished) account of real murders, a 'Kriminal-Novelle' (crime novella) by a Frank Heller was published.[19] The boundaries between fiction and fact blurred; serial murder and serial culture mirrored each other.

. . . .

The screenplay for *M* was finished before Kürten was arrested in May 1930, but his story, as it unfolded in the subsequent months, shadowed the production of the movie more than could have been foreseen. Kürten's psychiatric and forensic examination lasted from October 1930 to the end of January 1931, paralleling Lang's own preparation for *M*. Due to his confession, Kürten's trial lasted only ten days (from 13 April to 22 April 1931); it ended with the death penalty for murder in nine cases and attempted murder in seven others. Lang submitted his film to the Censorship Board on 27 April, only a few days after the end of Kürten's trial. *M*'s premiere on 11 May thus falls between Kürten's conviction in April and his execution in August.

It is not surprising that several critics considered *M* to be part of the flourishing Kürten industry. They spoke of Lang's 'Kürten-Film' and blamed it for capitalising – no less than other mass media – on mass murder.[20] No doubt Lang's own penchant for sensationalist and serial cinema was served by the horrid subject matter. He insisted that he did not want to glorify mass murder, but rather point out mass culture's problematic participation in what he called the 'mass murder complex'. In an article in 1931, Lang explained:

The epidemic series of mass murders of the last decade with their manifold and dark side effects had constantly absorbed me, as unappealing as their study may have been. It made me think of demonstrating, within the framework of a film story, the typical characteristics of this immense danger for the daily order and the ways of effectively fighting them. I found the prototype in the person of the Düsseldorf serial murderer and I also saw how here the side effects exactly repeated themselves, i.e. how they took on a typical form. I have distilled all typical events from the plethora of materials and combined them with the help of my wife into a self-contained film story. The film *M* should be a document and an extract of facts and in that way an authentic representation of a mass murder complex.[21]

What Lang refers to as the 'dark side effects' were the terrifying and thoroughly pernicious reactions of the masses to the public threat of serial murder. Although the murders happened near Düsseldorf, they stirred the imagination of the entire nation. Berlin's police detectives helped local officials and the Berlin papers reported about the events in the faraway Ruhr area as if they had happened in the capital itself. In addition, the well-known, charismatic Berlin police detective, Ernst Gennat (the prototype for inspector Karl Lohmann in *M*), was directly involved in solving the unsettling crimes that terrified a whole country for fifteen long months. What made the case unique was the public's intense preoccupation with the serial killings on a daily basis. Even odder was the fact that the murderer himself acted like a normal citizen who read with interest about his latest victims. Kürten wrote the police an anonymous letter detailing where he had buried one of his victims. When the police ignored the letter, he sent a copy to a newspaper, the Communist *Mittag*, on 14 November 1929, which published it in facsimile. Reprinted in all of the Reich's major newspapers, it caused further panic and a flood of fake letters from people claiming to be the murderer.

The pressure to apprehend the murderer, any murderer, led to the bizarre situation where a young man, Johann Stausberg, was put on trial in August 1929, after confessing to the murders. It soon became clear, however, that he only knew about the crimes from the sensational press reports. He was declared mentally deranged and committed to a psychiatric ward. The Stausberg fiasco demonstrated not only the impact of the press on unstable minds, but also the excessive public demand for a culprit. Supposedly more than 12,000 clues, leads and suggestions were reported to police and press by the general public; 300 so-called occultists and astrologists offered advice; and 200 persons called or wrote to confess the murders. Lang's film abounds with subtle and not-so-subtle references to this mass hysteria. When a colleague at Police Headquarters suggests that the public need to be more involved, Lohmann leaps to his feet: 'Don't talk to me about help from the general public. It disgusts me just to hear them talk … Good God! Has help from the public brought us one useful clue? … Just a pile of letters full of the most incredible accusations! … Calls to the police as soon as a chimney sweep crosses a yard.' In a missing scene (published in the appendix of this book), a person from Dresden, insisting he is the murderer, provides comic relief. Lohmann cuts him off and chides him for trying to finagle a free trip to Berlin out of this 'confession'.

Lang drew most heavily on Gennat's detailed articles published in the journal *Kriminalistische Monatshefte* between January and April 1930, while the search for the killer was still on. (Two more articles on the trial followed in May and June 1931.) Many telling details – for instance, the fact that the murderer's letter was written with a pencil on a wooden surface – appeared in Gennat's article as well as in *M*.[22] Whether or not Lang borrowed from Gennat is not important; explicit information about all aspects of the murders circulated widely. The killings themselves were known to the majority of the public in the form of news and special reports that read like crime fiction.

Gennat distinguishes three psychoses, which are also inscribed in Lang's *M*. First, the 'attack psychosis'. Stories about the serial killer, claimed Gennat, frightened the population to such a degree that they felt a curious readiness for the murderous attack to happen. To imagine a murderer's strike is almost like experiencing it. After each new murder, the police had to cope with an increasing number of false alarms. The washerwoman's tense command to the children to stop singing the 'damned murderer song' reflects this psychosis. By chanting a verse about the mass murderer's pending arrival, the children literally prepare themselves for it. Second, the so-called 'missing persons psychosis' gripped those who awaited loved ones. Had the mass murderer struck again? Mrs Beckmann's increasingly apprehensive and anxious glances at the clock when Elsie fails to come home in time re-enacts this collective panic. Finally, what Gennat calls the 'letter psychosis' is possibly the most disturbing effect; it refers to the mania of copycat letters written in the wake of Kürten's note to the newspaper. By March 1930, Gennat remarks with incredulity, no fewer than 160 letters were received from people who felt the need to make false confessions. Newspapers, believing they were real, initially printed them. Because Kürten's original missive appeared in facsimile, many copycat letters even imitated his handwriting. There was heavy competition among the various papers – each wanting to have the murderer as a 'regular correspondent', as Gennat sarcastically remarks. Murderer letters were the rage; with each new one, further copycat documents followed. Citizens responded to anonymous letters, telling the police they knew someone with that handwriting. Others wrote to private persons using the murderer's handwriting, seeking to scare them with murder threats. Most letters were easily recognised as fakes but the very fact that the police had to issue public warnings about these letters added to the atmosphere of collective distrust and paranoia.

Does Beckert, the suspected serial murderer, write a letter to the press (as Jack the Ripper and Kürten did) to put himself into the limelight? The film leaves this open as a possibility. Is Beckert's confession then to be understood in the context of 200 other confessions by 'wannabe' murderers? Eager to be lifted out of their obscure existence, they sought public notoriety. Yet breaking out of an existence as a mere serial number produced only copycats – how was one to escape seriality?[23]

The search for the serial killer Kürten was one of the first media-driven spectacles in Europe. Between thirty and forty journalists and photographers from all the major German papers, as well as correspondents from France and England, went to Düsseldorf to report from the frontlines about the war against the murderer. The telephone rang non-stop with reporters asking politely, as Gennat put it, 'whether a new child murder had occurred or was likely to occur'. The law of seriality had created the pressure to produce new murders.

. . . .

Although Kürten was the most articulate and self-reflexive among Weimar's serial killers, he was himself only one in a series. Georg Karl Grossmann, a butcher who made a living selling human flesh, was arrested in August 1921 after having killed and chopped up several prostitutes. He laughed when he was given the death penalty and hanged himself in jail. In December 1924, Karl Denke, a farmer and devout churchgoer, was discovered to have kept the pickled remains of thirty bodies of transients and drifters in his house. The most sensational case was that of Fritz Haarmann of Hannover, the first German serial killer (and Lang's Man in Black) whose trial generated widespread daily press reports and inspired numerous writers and artists. Haarmann stood accused of murdering twenty-seven young men within a six-year period from 1918 to 1924.

The trial of Haarmann introduced issues that are also at work in Lang's film: the question of the murderer's mental capacity; his compulsion to kill and the controversy about police and court procedures. Theodor Lessing, prolific journalist and professor of psychology in Hannover, wrote an impassioned book on the court case in 1925, entitled *Haarmann – the Story of a Werewolf*, a widely read treatise which castigates the court's handling of the case, especially its bloody retribution. Lang most certainly knew this account. Haarmann's physiognomy, for instance, resembled that of Lorre to a tee:

> Of average height, broad and well built, he had a coarse, rough, shiny full-moon face … the physiognomy was noticeably tight, 'trapped in the grip of the self', but at the same time he appeared to be unbelievably talkative, wanting sympathy and hyperactive. … His voice mushy, smarmy and close to a treble, was like the querulous voice of an old woman. His whole disposition was 'androgynous', not masculine or feminine and not child-like, but a combination of all three. [24]

In and out of prison from early on, Haarmann was frequently transferred to clinics and asylums after pleading insanity (Paragraph 51). When the lynch mob at the end of *M* scoffs at Paragraph 51 being applied in the case of the child murderer, they remember how Haarmann escaped from the asylum to continue his murderous spree. 'And what if the compulsion to kill returns?' asks Schränker. 'Yet another man-hunt for several months. Paragraph 51 again. Into the asylum again and then another escape or release. And then the compulsion all over again. And so on till doomsday.' In his trial, Haarmann often pleaded in a manner similar to the suspected murderer in *M*: 'Often, after I had killed, I pleaded to be put away in a military asylum, but not in a madhouse.… Oh, believe me, I'm not ill. It's only that I occasionally have funny turns' (p. 82).

Lessing insists that the Haarmann case had more to do with 'the criticism of civilisation and psychiatry than with the law' (p. 128). He was the first to compare the mass murder of war with the serial killing of the postwar era. Relating the 'massacre of millions, the thieving, plundering, lying and spying perpetrated during the so-called "great periods of history"' to the crimes of individuals, he insists that people share guilt rather than take revenge. Lessing wanted the murderer to be seen in a social context: 'The further the trial progresses,' he wrote, 'the more obvious it became that it is impossible to judge a snake without also putting the marsh from which the snake obtained its nourishment on trial' (p. 124). And he continued: 'Nature did not create the evil monsters. They were created by the cage.... our madhouses cause madness, our prisons create criminals' (p. 139). Both Kürten and Haarmann had served lengthy prison terms before they became serial killers. Haarmann was found guilty of twenty-four murders (he claimed to have killed many more) and executed by guillotine on 4 April 1925. Lang's *M* is one of a series of cultural responses, from nursery rhymes to paintings and films, that have kept Haarmann's memory alive.[25]

. . . .

The law of seriality which drove Kürten and Haarmann to kill by numbers informs the very structure of Lang's *M*. It is different from his other films in that it presents an accumulation of autonomous scenes held together not by an overt cause-and-effect logic, but by the principle of illustration and seriality. For example, in a scene reminiscent of early cinema in which a lecturer stood next to the screen commenting on the film's various locales and activities, the police commissioner, on the phone with the minister, explains the police's investigative procedures. The screen accompanies his commentary with a succession of vignettes about detective work: interrogating a couple, questioning a shopgirl, combing a garden plot, picking up a piece of candy wrapping, etc. Over these silent and brief skits, the voice continues to explain what we see. The effect of this sequence comes close to that of a documentary about police procedure – a public relations film in the spirit of the highly popular Police Exhibition held in Berlin in 1926, which proudly displayed the latest detection and surveillance equipment. Lang and Harbou may actually have seen films used by the Berlin police for training purposes when they did field research at the 'Alex', Berlin's gigantic police headquarters at the Alexanderplatz. After the raid of an underworld bar, the film painstakingly takes stock of a huge arsenal of guns, knives and stolen goods – the astounding spoils of a simple foray into the criminal realm, physical evidence over which the camera pans across in a medium close-up. The film assumes the police's perspective, as if to record for posterity their superhuman crime-fighting efforts. This fascination with reportage and realistic detail shows the influence of the New Objectivity movement and its belief in irrefutable facts.

The serial narrative had a further function: it allowed a proliferation of autonomous scenes, which disregard the unity of time and place, and often merely visualise and illustrate what is said – as if Lang, coming from silent film, would not trust words alone. These brief scenes germinate (one leading to another) and create an intricate network of news, messages, advertisements, posters, announcements, commentaries and rumours – all encoded in a written, visual or aural form. According to the law of seriality, every message generates more messages, just as every bogus letter to the press in Kürten's case was followed by more copycat letters, all equally bogus. *M* mimics this phenomenon in its excessive array of multiple interlocked and doubly embedded scenes. These do not follow a narratively bound chronology, but the spatial expanse of fragmentary information which corresponds to an explosion of viewpoints. Everything counts – the police commissioner says that sixty volumes of evidence have been gathered and 1500 leads have been followed; every little detail might be the missing piece in the puzzle. The city is shown as an echo chamber in which information is incessantly exchanged by word of mouth, by reading the papers and by telephone. While the film's structure in its presentational *gestus* and epic sweep (not fixated on characters, but focused on the context that shapes them) resembles Brecht's Epic Theatre, Lang's project is ultimately a different one. Less interested in leftist political matters than Brecht, Lang probes the status and function of visual communication in a modern urban environment which is dominated by an insatiable hunger for news and information. Why, for instance, is the break-in into the office building shown twice? First we witness it filmed in (almost) real time, then depicted as a series of photographs taken at the crime scene and included in a detailed police report. Lohmann studies this report and comments on the photographs which depict what we have already seen in live action. This doubling of representation – the action and its record – makes the viewer realise the limits of the visible. Looking at the crime pictures, which are presented in the photo-journalistic style of

Ironic seriality

1931 tabloids, Lohmann admits not to understand at all what the isolated photographs mean. (What were the criminals after if no money was stolen?) Pictures show surfaces but not the story behind them.

Subtly but insistently, Lang puts an ironic spin on seriality as a modern means of controlling excess and confusion. A beggar is shown in close-up sorting about fifty cigar and cigarette butts according to size; the chef of the beggar's kitchen counts and organises his sausages and sand-wiches. Small-time crooks stand in line waiting to be questioned, one after another, by Lohmann. One of them, wearing an elegant fur coat, carries a newspaper with a report on a recent fur store burglary, which immediately gives him away. The scene provides a succinct and ironic clue for the film's message about the rapid circulation between events and their representation – and its price.

Lang was never a stranger to seriality. He began writing film scripts for early adventure and crime serials popular in World War I. Lang's early film *Die Spinnen* (The Spiders, 1919) has two parts, as do his *Nibelungen* (1924) and his films set in India (1959). He continued his two-part crime film *Dr. Mabuse, the Gambler* (1922) with a third, *Das Testament des Dr. Mabuse* (The Testament of Dr. Mabuse, 1933), which immediately fol-lowed *M*. As if to bring the point home, he added another sequel, *Die tausend Augen des Dr. Mabuse* (The Thousand Eyes of Dr. Mabuse) in 1959, his last German film.

Lang's *M* becomes part of the serial murder series in its very first scene, which begins with a folksy appropriation of Haarmann's story. The 'man in black', as the nursery rhyme calls him, lives on in myth and folklore; serial culture cannot let him die. The rhyme, which we hear three times at the beginning of the film, expresses a fascination with seriality and its deadly logic: the murderer will kill in an orderly fashion, one victim after another, but eventually he will come around to kill you, too. Elimination is the flip side of seriality. The children have turned this macabre nursery rhyme into a ritual of exclusion ('You are out') that perfectly encapsulates the intertwining of serial murder and serial culture.

3
....

TOTAL MOBILISATION

A studio street. The camera frames a police poster which reads '10,000 Marks Reward. Who is the Murderer?' It slowly pulls back, revealing adjacent posters advertising a boxing match, a comedy stage, a circus, a dance school and a movie theatre showing *Spreewaldmädel*, a popular film at the time. Serial murder had become part of mass culture, qualified to compete with nightly entertainment, with which it shares its serial nature. Detection itself had also become a form of mass entertainment. In 1926, for instance, the police challenged the population to a well-publicised game of finding a person they had sent into the streets with distinguishing marks. There were prizes for the winners. An early silent film, *Wo ist Coletti?* (Where is Coletti?, 1913), showed an entire metropolis searching for a person eager to prove that he could disappear in the city streets. The idea was to train the urban masses to look with a

Murder as media event

sharper eye at their surroundings and, in the spirit of heightened self-surveillance, quickly register deviation and difference.

As the camera pulls back farther, a crowd congregating in front of the billboard pillar becomes visible, shoving and jostling each other as they try to get a closer look at the small print on the poster. A clatter of voices is heard, some expressing shock and disbelief, others demanding that those in front read the small-printed text of the poster aloud. Only fragments are audible: 'The terror in our town has found a new ... victim ... Louder, we can't hear a thing ...' Reading about the child murderer on the police poster gives the crowd a curious rush; they cannot get enough. This commotion also recalls the excitement during the first days of the war (captured by photographs and documentary film) when the latest news reports were posted hourly on billboards and distributed as extra editions.

As the camera dollies back in an overhead shot, we see mostly men with hats and overcoats, their backs turned to the camera to emphasise their anonymity. They all look the same, a highly mobile and volatile mass of nameless figures, any one of them a possible murderer. In fact, the child murderer himself might be among the crowd standing in the front of the poster, inexorably drawn to the news, at once shocked and mesmerised: 'And afterwards I see those posters,' Beckert confesses at the end, 'and I read what I've done ... I read ... and ... and read ... Did I do that?' Reading about his crimes seems to give him additional pleasure, a pleasure he shares with a million others fantasising about crime and transgression. The scene in front of the billboard shows an agitated crowd ready to let rumour and suggestion transform them into an angry mob. The frame, even though it expands as the camera backtracks, can hardly contain the ever-growing crowd.

Amidst the cacophony, one loud, high-pitched voice becomes dominant, but it is not yet identifiable as the camera lingers over the crowd. Cut indoors to a barroom where an older gentleman reads aloud from a newspaper to his five drinking companions assembled around a table. It was his voice we heard. This sound bridge demonstrates the ubiquity of the news transmitted by sound. The voice, disembodied at first, could easily have been that of a radio, carrying the news everywhere, disregarding distinctions between outside and inside, public and private. The sound continues while the locales change, connecting the diverse spaces and constituting the city as one complex body united and energised by an unceasing flow of information.

The barroom scene is claustrophobic. Shot again from above, with a spidery ceiling lamp covering the top of the frame, it depicts a *Stammtisch* gathering of friends (exclusively males at that time) in a bar. Their grotesque physiques are modelled after George Grosz's savage caricatures of the self-satisfied, war-mongering German bourgeoisie around World War I. They consume the latest titillating news of the child murderer, as they consume their beer and cigars. The camera cuts to two men eyeing each other, as the reading continues off screen: 'What is he like? Where is he hiding? No one knows. And, yet, he is one of us. Your neighbour could be the murderer.' 'Why are you looking at me,' asks one of them. Within seconds they are at each other's throats, one barking 'You murderer' and the other screaming 'slanderer'. The camera dramatises the aggression through rapid cross-cutting between the two combatants,

Beer, cigars and murder

both wild-eyed and crazed, before returning to its high-angle point of departure, coldly observing how the detection mania ('Who is the murderer?') destroys friendship and community.

The last word of this disturbing scene, 'slanderer', is repeated by a crying middle-aged woman as the film cuts to an apartment undergoing a house search, occasioned, as we learn, by an anonymous letter. The trench-coated police officer explains that he is only doing his duty: 'The police must follow every lead ... any man in the street ... could be the guilty man.' At the word 'street', the camera cuts to an overhead shot of a nocturnal street, where a distinguished-looking old gentleman, wearing a bowler hat and spectacles, waits for a bus and reads the newspaper. A little girl on a scooter enters the frame, asking him the time. The camera cuts away to two housewives and a burly workman, who immediately intervenes when the old man responds to the girl. A heated exchange ensues, caricatured with distorted camera angles: the extreme high angle dwarfs the old man, while the workman, shot from an extremely low angle, towers over him. The camera comments on the power relationship between accuser and accused by exaggerating their mutual subjective perception and by adding a comic touch that highlights the absurdity of the suspicion.

The altercation draws a crowd and the old man suddenly finds himself under suspicion of being the child murderer. 'You wanted to take off with her, didn't you?' asks the workman. Bystanders scream 'Punch his face in' and 'It's the murderer! It's him!' As they call for police, a double-decker bus enters the frame. A policeman appears with a pickpocket in tow who protests loudly that the police ought to look for the child murderer instead of harrassing petty thieves like him. The crowd only hears 'child murderer' and starts pressing against the bus, shouting and shrieking: 'That's him ... the murderer!' In the general confusion, the mob shifts its ire to the pickpocket. It does not matter who he is, as long as a scapegoat is found. This scene shows the making of a mob which overwhelms the police as well as the camera. The camera's eye-level position emphasises the chaos; it becomes part of the rabble, shuffling and scuffling in search of the prey which is ultimately no longer visible. This series of tableaux, linked by editing, chronicles a frightening escalation: it starts with a bar-room brawl and ends with mass contagion. From scene to scene, distinctions between fact and rumour, suspicion and guilt, civility and violence collapse. Lang's montage shows how mistrust, suspicion and fear collude to create collective hysteria.

. . . .

The ease with which a group of faceless citizens became a mobilised mass triggered associations of World War I. In August 1914, the entire German nation quickly united to take on 'a world of enemies'. Lang subtly alludes to this memory when his moving camera catches a glimpse of two identical movie posters side by side, advertising the most celebrated German war film at the time, G. W. Pabst's *Westfront 1918*. We see the posters only for a split second as a man with a young girl walks by a wall, suspiciously observed by a beggar/spy wearing a bogus sign reading 'Blind' around his neck. Is the man a father with his daughter or the child murderer with a new victim? The beggar does his duty; he surveys the urban battlefield.

The spectre of the war

The allusion to *Westfront 1918*, released exactly a year prior to *M*, served as a temporal marker to emphasise once more the topicality of the movie. It was probably also an industry in-joke, because Pabst's film and *M* were both produced by Nero-Film. But Lang's explicit reference to a war film (he could have chosen other contemporary Nero film posters) gestures towards a more profound nexus between the two films, despite their seemingly different topographies. Is *M*'s Berlin not presented as a 'Westfront 1931', a city in a state of total mobilisation prepared to fight an enemy who had invaded the community?

Overt references to the war experience abounded at the time. 'War in Düsseldorf' screamed the headline of an article in the *Berliner Morgenpost* on 25 November 1929, which detailed the serial murderer's impact on the community:

> All doors are locked, window shades are drawn, no woman, no child would dare to step outside the fortress of their home into the death front of the nightly street. One finds only men in the bars and there is nobody who doesn't have a weapon in his pocket. There is war in Düsseldorf. War of the minds, hearts and fists against the beast in human shape. Against a terrible enemy who cannot be caught, against a master of black magic who remains invisible, shadow-like, spectral. It is a war against a human being that possesses nothing human. It is a war against a phantom.

The enemy as beast and phantom: this vocabulary also reached back to

World War I. A flood of war novels, memoirs and picture books, from the far right to the far left, inundated the book market at the time. Erich Maria Remarque's 1929 novel *Im Westen nichts Neues* (All Quiet on the Western Front) was the most popular, with more than one million copies sold. In December 1930, the American film adaptation of Remarque's book provoked riots in Berlin. Nationalist forces considered the film a defamation of Germany and succeeded in having it banned until cuts were made. Ernst Jünger's philosophical essay 'Total Mobilisation', which also appeared in 1930, reconfigured the war in terms of labour, discipline and social order. And Lang's *M* contributed in its own way to the trend: it demonstrated the extent to which the war experience was re-enacted in a repetition compulsion which for Freud was a symptom of trauma.

In *M*, Lang alludes to scenes well known from war films. The raid on the basement bar, a hangout for criminals, is staged and shot like a military operation. From extreme high angle, the camera observes columns of uniformed and armed police advancing in locked step, reminiscent of infantry marching in formation. Later, one of the gangsters surveys the scene from the same angle through binoculars, as if reconnoitring the enemy's position.

The war was still a living memory in 1931. Lang singles out Emil Dustermann from the long line of nameless beggars as the embodiment of the classical veteran. His wooden leg signifies that he was one of the millions of soldiers who returned from the front as invalids. Limbs were often blown off as grenades and shells exploded, or amputated because of a lack of surgical facilities in front hospitals. These cripples who dotted the streets of Weimar as solemn reminders of the war found themselves outsiders in a

War cripple at the home front

society which sought to repress the national shame of defeat and resented the financial and moral burden veterans imposed. It was not uncommon for war cripples to end up playing the hurdy-gurdy in tenement courtyards, selling papers or balloons, or joining the ever growing army of beggars. Emil Dustermann stands for the continuity between the trenches and the domestic front more than a decade later. In a scene reminiscent of millions of volunteers registering for military service in August 1914, the camera captures the bureaucratic particulars of induction: Dustermann's name and post are meticulously recorded in a close-up of pedantic handwriting. 'Dustermann, Emil' receives a carbon copy of the record.

. . . .

In 'Total Mobilisation', Ernst Jünger argued that the general process of militarisation and mobilisation necessitated by the war did not cease in 1918.[26] Manifest signs of total mobilisation in World War I ranged from the large number of volunteers and reservists to the management of raw materials; from censorship to the fusion of military and political command; from the curtailment of individual liberty to subordination of everything to the dictates of the state. Because war was no longer fought between professional or volunteer armies, distinctions between soldiers and civilians, between 'armies that meet on the battle fields' and 'modern armies of commerce and transport', lost their meaning according to Jünger. Everyone was involved in the war effort – resulting in new technologies of supervision, registration and surveillance which remained (and even expanded) once the war was over.

In *M*, an entire city mobilises itself to wage all-out war against the child murderer. Every resource is activated; differences in class and social status become irrelevant. The editing underscores the mobilisation through seamless cross-cuts between the strategy session of the police and the meeting of the underworld. Sentences begun in one setting are completed in the other. The leader of the crime syndicate continues a hand movement begun by the police president. Both meetings, sites of concentrated thinking and heated debate, are enshrouded in heavy clouds of smoke which make the two spaces all but indistinguishable. While the editing establishes the common goal – the capture of the child murderer – thick smoke blurs differences of status and position. Smoking among men establishes a curious commonality which even includes Beckert, who betrays himself by leaving three cigarette butts at the crime scene as evidence. In addition, smoking

A gesture begun by the master
criminal …

… is continued, in a match-
cut, by the chief of police

Criminals as phantoms

triggered associations of the war (or, more precisely, the war film), where the consumption of cigarettes was a means to combat anxiety. Not surprisingly, Schränker, the most callous of all, does not smoke, while Lohmann, expansive and compassionate, is unimaginable without his cigar. *M*'s inordinate focus on smoking points to a society under unbearable stress.

Mobilisation makes visible the tightly woven web of controls already in place. Criminals and vagrants have identity papers (as the film shows, forgeries are easily detected), they are registered and monitored, their fingerprints are recorded and analysed with the latest technology.[27] (The Berlin Police had more than a million fingerprints on file in 1930.) Asylums and hospitals keep medical records. Telephone lines link the population to the authorities, and office buildings maintain alarm systems connected to police headquarters. Plain-clothes detectives search in widening circles for every possible irregularity; neighbours watch each other; parents train their children to be wary and every person in the street is seen as a potential suspect. Newspapers and extra editions keep the public current at all times. Not only photography and film, but also law, medicine, architecture and pedagogy had, for more than a decade, been tirelessly involved in improving techniques and technologies of surveillance.

With a relentlessly panoptic resolve and detached 'cold gaze', the camera itself becomes a participant in the process of mobilisation. It emulates the police and the underworld – it surveys the terrain and tracks the suspect. The relationship between the camera and the policing eye is repeatedly invoked. When Beckert walks into a street café, the camera, like a detective, lurks behind the trellis. As Beckert leaves, the camera pulls back with a jolt as if it wanted to escape detection. To be effective in surveillance, the camera itself must remain invisible.

Schränker's plot to catch the child murderer is to occupy the city with an invisible army of spies, enlisting them to observe all citizens at all times. He says: 'Every square inch must be under constant surveillance. No child may take an unnoticed step.' Instead of resolving a crime after it is committed, which is the method of the police, the underworld opts for crime prevention. The price, of course, is high: total surveillance and mobilisation, a voluntary fascism motivated by fear of violence.

Who can be stationed in the streets and remain invisible? As soon as Schränker answers his own question – 'the beggars!' – the scene shifts to the beggar's union headquarters, where his plan is already being implemented. The abrupt cut and implied time ellipsis underscores the

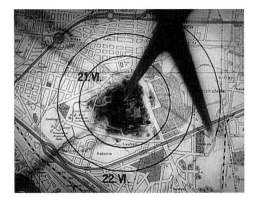

Cartography as surveillance …

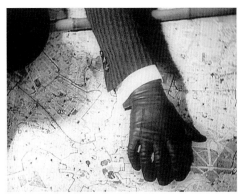

… and capture

impressive power of Schränker and his gang to impose their will as soon as the decision is made. In iconography reminiscent of Pabst's rendering of Brecht's *Threepenny Opera* (which had opened only three months earlier), Lang's film finds beauty in the simple but offbeat life of the beggars. The highly mobile camera (apparently hand-held) explores the large space of the beggars' meeting place, using uncoordinated quick pans to focus on some colourful detail and conveying a sense of picturesque authenticity. The corpulent boss of the Beggars' Market yanks a steaming sausage from a pot and takes a bite, then he counts sandwiches in twos – he is obviously preparing food for the troops of beggars en route to their surveillance posts. The camera pans up to a huge blackboard reading 'Prices for the Evening of the 16th'. In a parody of the stockmarket (which had crashed less than two years before), the fluctuating prices for every sort of sandwich are listed. Comical touches abound: from the signs on the wall of the Beggars' Union – 'No Credit Given' and 'Begging Not Allowed' – to their obsessively scrupulous bookkeeping. Bureaucratisation has percolated down to the lowest strata of society, a passive mobilisation, as it were, which keeps a tight grip on everyone and everything.

The camera pans up to an upstairs makeshift office where beggars wait in line (a motley group which includes a dwarf) to receive their street assignment. Schränker, dapper in a leather coat and with a cane, stands by and watches. An insert shot of a street map marks the places where children have been murdered. A subsequent series of shots shows the various places where the beggars are stationed. Facilitated by telephone, telegraph, press and radio, the city under surveillance has become a complex communication and information network, a fully transparent and rationalised collective.

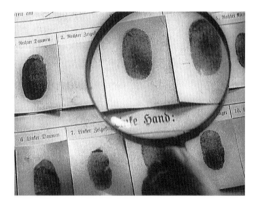

Technologies of investigation and classification

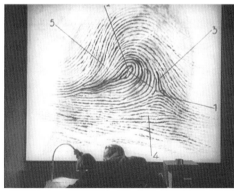

The film's obsession with surveillance also addresses the deep-seated fear of an expanding urban population. The ease with which Beckert was able to hide, even after he had been branded by the sign 'M', must have scared the contemporary audience. Berlin more than doubled in population by the end of the decade; it had reached 4.5 million inhabitants in 1930. Attempts to control and discipline these masses included insistent endeavours to survey, classify, categorise and supervise them. Vision and surveillance foster discipline and control. 'Traditionally,' writes Foucault in *Discipline and Punish*, 'power was what was seen ... disciplinary power, on the other hand, is exercised through its invisibility. ... It is the fact of being constantly seen, of being able always to be seen, that maintains the disciplined individual in his subjection.'[28] For Foucault, the perfect disciplinary apparatus enables a single gaze to see everything all the time. For Lang, however, even a single panoptic gaze could not comprehend, let alone discipline and contain, the psychopathological Beckert. While Lang examines the nexus between total mobilisation, surveillance and social control, he also insists on an unknowable remainder, a scintilla of resistance which defies categorisation.

. . . .

The return to war in literature and film of the late 1920s and early 1930s was itself a symptom for an increasingly militarised political reality. Private quasi-armies and militant commandos of the extreme right and left engaged in what the Nazis called the 'politics of the street'. The psychological wounds of the lost war and the Treaty of Versailles still festered beneath the democratic surface, as if the battles had been carried from the front into the midst of German society. In 1931, one could readily view the pursuit of the child murderer as a war between organised crime and the police. Excluded in this struggle was the government, represented by the Minister, who is far removed from the action. He appears only once in the film, calling from an unknown location, complaining about the public relations disaster of the unresolved murder case. The police president must remind him of the citizens' right to write letters to the press as they wish. When the Minister becomes impatient, he is politely rebuffed: 'Herr Minister, you do not seem to understand ...' – a phrase that sums up the film's sceptical, even dismissive attitude towards governmental help. The over-eager general public is also shown to be useless. Inspector Lohmann denigrates it with venom and disdain as a bunch of slanderers and ignoramuses. The police president laments that no fewer than fifteen witnesses have given contradictory accounts of Elsie's walk home from school. A cutaway (listed as 'testimony 1478') shows two of them at a police station. They are unable to agree about the colour of Elsie's cap, shouting each other down, while the camera exposes their agitated faces and staccato voices: 'It was red, Inspector.' 'No, it was green.' 'Red.' 'Green.' 'Red.' 'Green.' The camera exaggerates the comedy by cutting between them more and more rapidly. This comical scene undermines any hope for concrete assistance from the public at large.

Help would come from battle plans. Lang shows two competing strategies and it is part of the film's viewing pleasure to watch which of the two will triumph. Will it be the police under the command of the jovial and cunning Inspector Lohmann, who (at least at first) enters the urban battlefield like Sherlock Holmes, looking for clues and relying on logic and reason? Or will it be the crime syndicate under the leadership of Schränker, the criminal with class, who decides to seize the city and place it under total surveillance? Lang captures the two operations by showing the same city map twice. While the police draw concentric circles around the crime site, signifying the methodical procedures of their ever-widening investigation, Schränker puts his black-gloved hand over the map, suggesting force and terror.

Organised crime in Weimar was a central part of Berlin's urban scene, open and widespread, feared but tolerated. At the core were the so-called *Ringvereine* (ring clubs), gang-like organisations (not unlike Chicago's Mafia) and a shadow police force that 'protected' businesses in exchange for extortion money. They controlled the entire semi-criminal underworld – prostitution, gambling and drugs – and they also lorded over Weimar Berlin's world-famous decadent nightlife, a huge industry. They ran the beggars' union, controlled the sale of guns and managed 'professional' break-ins. Originally founded in 1890 as social organisations for ex-convicts, their numbers swelled after the economic depression. In 1929, more than fifty groups were joined in a central 'Ring' for Berlin. They sported colourful and ironic names such as 'Evergreen' and 'Forget-Me-Not'. They could afford the best lawyers in town and provided an ongoing source of urban entertainment in their mostly non-violent struggles with the police. (It was part of their lore that they would avoid murder – Lohmann uses this to his advantage when he interrogates Franz, the hapless criminal left behind in the break-in.) Organised crime inspired writers and film-makers, providing, as in Brecht's *Threepenny Opera*, an only slightly distorted mirror of society. It was a sign of class among Berlin's bohème to be associated with them. Gustav Gründgens, who plays Schränker in *M*, was in fact an honorary member of one of these ring organisations.

Structured like small companies, with a charismatic figure as leader (Schränker with gloves and a cane, or Mackie Messer in Pabst's *3-Groschen-Oper*) and with strict rules (penalties for missed meetings, for instance) and procedures (Schränker runs his meeting with representatives from various ring clubs like a manager), these ring clubs clearly resembled legitimate businesses. As Lang's film illustrates, the police ventured into the underworld only in times of crisis, after a particularly daring heist or in response to public pressure. The papers, ever hungry for sensational news, ran vivid reports about crimes, making heroes of both criminals and detectives. Police and underworld had become players on the public stage, locked in an ongoing cat-and-mouse game.

Lang appealed to the public's enjoyment of crime culture when he modelled his break-in into the office building after the stunning and widely publicised coup carried out by the Saas Brothers in 1929. These master criminals had cut a hole through the ceiling of the safe deposit area of Berlin's Disconto Bank, gaining access to valuable jewellery and coins. (Most of the loot was not claimed as loss by the owners for fear of being charged with tax evasion.) Despite a lengthy police investigation, hard evidence was lacking to convict the brothers. The public relished the battle between the ultra-cool thieves and the convivial but ill-starred police inspector. Upon their release, the brothers and their clever lawyer held a press conference, celebrating the defeat of authority with champagne – unwittingly providing further fodder for Joseph Goebbels' propaganda mill, which continually accused Berlin's police president of being incompetent and soft on crime. (The fear of police ineptitude also drives *M*.) The sympathies of the public lay by and large with the master criminals. Lang shows, in an admiring touch, a professional break-in artist loosening his fingers like a pianist, as he readies to pick a lock. Berlin's most brilliant lawyers were eager for publicity's sake to defend the underworld, if it came to a trial at all. As a saying went: 'You become "frei" if you come to Dr Frey' – a pun on the word *frei*, (i.e. free) and a reference to Dr Frey, a prominent defence lawyer for organised crime in Berlin. It was part of the criminal chic (and maybe the beginning of today's intertwining of law and mass culture) that Frey has a bit part in *M*: he plays a gangster.

. . . .

The police, underfunded and reduced in numbers as a result of the Versailles Treaty, tried hard to overcome their authoritarian image and to gain the sympathy of the public. In December 1929, for instance, the Berlin police president invited the public to mingle with the officers at a police ball. The public, so unusually wooed, responded by wanting to help the police whenever possible. They became amateur detectives, spies and informers – a development Lang's film condemns in no uncertain terms. Hitler's police state profited from a highly self-policing society being already in place.

Police Inspector Lohmann represents the prototype of a detective whose class and status were not so far removed from the small-time crooks whom he supervised. As the film demonstrates, a 'working' relationship between underworld and police developed in which Lohmann played a stern but fair and understanding father to his unruly (and only slightly transgressive) children. His large body ungainly, his clothes rumpled, his appearance unkempt, he addresses the crowd of small-time crooks and prostitutes at the raid: 'Come on now, children. Let's be reasonable.' The gangsters in turn call him Papa Lohmann. He remains unruffled, even jolly as he deals with everyday criminality, displaying his superiority vis-à-vis folks who have forged IDs. The camera, in the meantime, explores the various hiding places: one man emerges from behind the counter; another, slightly embarrassed, from the women's bathroom. None escapes. The police are shown to be efficient in their normal operations – as if to highlight the insuperable difficulties they have, by contrast, with the anonymous child murderer. In the style of a police education film, *M* shows the result of the raid: the camera pans slowly over an amazing array of tools (a leather briefcase containing a complete housebreaking kit is opened for a camera close-up) and a large assortment of weapons. Lang is fond of such inventory shots (we see similar ones after the office building break-in); they reinforce the film's documentary dimension and hint at the astonishing size of the underworld's semi-military arsenal.

The film does not allow identification with Inspector Lohmann. Although he elicits sympathy as a dedicated folksy detective who eats and sleeps in his office, several scenes interrupt any closer alignment. An extremely low-angle shot displays a distorted view of his legs and genitalia, a repulsive perspective that undermines any authority and dignity he might have possessed. It comes at the lowest point in his investigation, after the identity of the murderer has been established, but the culprit seems to have vanished. The camera suggests that the futile

Lohmann under siege

search for the child murderer has taken a physical toll; appearances no longer matter to him. When he hears that the underworld has caught the killer, his cigar drops from his mouth. But when the gangster's information offers a lucky break, he goes to a washroom and puts his head under the faucet. The progress of the investigation registers itself on his body.

Lohmann is also shown to break the law when it furthers his cause. He scares Franz with a bogus murder charge to force a confession. In a brief cutaway, we see the guard, supposedly dead, enjoying a huge meal of blood sausage and wheat beer. Using Heinrich Zille, the popular caricaturist and photographer of the Berlin milieu, as his guide, Lang often indulges in Berliniana in this film – a powerful counterforce here to his otherwise abstract tendencies. The editing reveals that Lohmann is lying, fabricating a murder charge, which the omniscient camera immediately repudiates. Lohmann's violation of the law parallels Schränker's torture of a guard who refuses to cooperate. The film shows how both sides break the law in their pursuit of the murderer. The city – like Germany itself under Heinrich Brüning in 1931 – was no longer governed by rule of law, but swayed by the pressure of the mobilised masses.

4
· ·
BEFORE THE LAW

What does a serial killer look like? Gazing at himself in the mirror, Beckert distorts his face and grimaces. Why? To see if his visage could be recognised as that of a child murderer? Or to give himself the image that others might have of a criminal? This confrontation with his mirror image – an 18-second-long take that was cut from the shorter version – is important for understanding not only the murderer's self-fashioning, but also the nexus of self-examination and interiorised surveillance that informs the entire film.

The scene reveals Beckert's face for the first time. Shot in medium close-up, slightly from below so as to include him and his mirror image, the scene splits and doubles his face, raising a host of questions about identity, performance and cinematic representation. Is it Lorre or Beckert, played by Lorre, who is mirrored in the film? Is there one body too many? The double perspective literalises Beckert's split personality ('It's me, pursuing myself ...') and self-reflexively points to the act of seeing. The scene itself is doubly embedded within two other narratives: it is a cut-away from a handwriting expert analysing Beckert's letter to the press, a brief scene which itself is inserted in a telephone conversation between the police commissioner and the minister about police detection methods. On a narrative level, the complexly encased 'mirror scene' underscores the degree to which Beckert is 'boxed in'. He is doubly 'covered' and constituted by two regimes: the socio-political (government/police) and the scientific (physiognomy/graphology). Both are incessantly at work to observe, record, characterise and categorise the subject.

The scene begins with a graphology expert dictating a report to a female secretary, while pacing back and forth in front of a wall that is covered from floor to ceiling with hundreds of identical files – a commentary on the overwhelming bureaucratic setting that recalls Kafka's depiction of a nightmarish legal system in his 1925 posthumously published novel *Der Prozeß* (The Trial). The camera is deliberately immobile to stress the rigid milieu. The expert, who wears dark glasses and speaks in a stentorian voice, 'overshoots' the frame and goes outside it for a few seconds – a comical touch that undercuts the overconfidence of scientific inquiry. By not following him, the camera suggests that he ignores his boundaries (his 'frame'), just as he ignores the limits of his pseudo-science, which had a huge following at the time. (Ludwig Klages' 1907 book on handwriting and character had gone through numerous editions and was enormously popular in the late 1920s.) The graphologist classifies Beckert's handwriting:

The form of his writing registers the pathologically strong sexuality of this person with uncontrollable impulses and drives. The

Play-acting or madness?

broken style of his letters is a sign of play-acting which could express indolence or apathy. In the sample there is an elusive but conspicuous quality of madness.

As the expert dictates this report, the film first cuts away to a brief insert shot of the handwriting in extreme close-up, then to Beckert in front of a mirror. It cuts to him precisely at the word 'play-acting' (*Schauspielerei*); and returns to the scene with the police chief at the word 'madness' (*Wahnsinn*). Beckert's 'problem' is thus framed between play-acting and madness, between simulation and illness. When he looks at himself in the mirror, Beckert is indeed 'acting'. He uses his middle fingers to contort his lips and pull down the corners of his mouth. As the word 'madness' is uttered, he looks to the side, bulging his eyes and exhibiting a truly frightening visage. Beckert is defined (more precisely, constituted and controlled) by two schools of physiognomy: by his handwriting and by the shape and expression of his face. By disfiguring his face, he manipulates his appearance so that it coincides with the image that criminological science (informed by physiognomy) already has of him as a madman and criminal. A number of physiognomists of the nineteenth century – above all, Cesare Lombroso and Francis Galton – had argued that criminals had a recognisable look and were biologically predestined to be '*L'Uomo Delinquente*', as Lombroso entitled his influential book in 1876. Scientists in the nineteenth century photographed, measured, grouped, compared, cross-referenced and catalogued thousands of faces to develop a physiognomy of the aberrant and dangerous. Classificatory schemes for identifying (and isolating) deviance became necessary as the urban population grew by leaps and bounds. But what do child murderers look like? Could it be anybody? Or are there facial characteristics that make them stand out?

'There is no such thing as a murderer's visage', declared Lang in a little-known essay, entitled 'The Face of the Murderer' and tellingly published in *Tempo*, a Berlin tabloid, to coincide with the opening of *M*. (In the film it is *Tempo* that publishes Beckert's letter!) The criminal physiognomy does not exist, according to Lang, 'serial killers like Grossmann and Haarmann could live next door to their neighbors without raising even a trace of suspicion.' This statement appears almost verbatim in *M*. Lang observes:

> None of Kürten's victims could have divined the unparalleled degeneracy of this man by looking at his face.… All famous mass

murderers were flesh from our flesh, blood from our blood ... In the film *M* one woman says to the other: 'But he doesn't look like a murderer!' To which another says: 'That's the terrible thing about it.' And another adds with a warning: 'Anyone next to you could be the murderer!'[29]

Since Beckert shows no outward signs of deviation – at least not at first sight – how can one recognise him? Criminological theories based on physiognomy, suggests Lang, have become tools of self-examination and self-surveillance. Lorre's grimace belies the notion of an innate and fixed criminal identity.

. . . .

While Lang emphasises here Beckert's elusive normality, in the film he systematically isolates him. Crucially, he makes Lorre effeminate, childlike and diminutive, given to oral fixation (eating fruit in public) and with an intense fascination with objects in store windows. The assonance of his name with that of his victim (Beckert/Beckmann) intimates an affinity and points to a paradox: his closeness to children allows him to assume the role of a substitute father – one girl calls him 'uncle' – in this postwar world bereft of fathers. (Except for one criminal, none of the men seems to be married or to have children; we never see any of them in a domestic setting.) In fact, every man on the street, unless he is a criminal or beggar, is under suspicion of being the child murderer. This problematic economy of gender provides a striking comment on the strained relations between the sexes after the war and on the disastrous impact of material conditions on traditional family structures.

Even before the famous 'M' in white chalk is stamped on his shoulder, Beckert had caught the eye of the law. Lohmann hypothesises:

> The guilty man or the possible suspect must already have a record somewhere. A man that disturbed must have fallen foul of the law before. We've got to contact every clinic, every prison, every lunatic asylum. We'll have to make inquiries about everyone who has been freed as harmless, but who has the same pathological condition as the killer.

Soon after, Lohmann receives a list of former mental patients who have been released during the past five years. In close-up (once again illustrating the film's fascination with documentation), we see a series of typewritten reports with such letterheads as 'Dr Goll's Psychiatric Institution' or 'Professor Emil Lebbowitz's Private Clinic for Mental Patients'. 'Reports from every institution, private and public', an assistant says off camera. Lohmann scans an additional list of the present addresses of former mental patients. We surmise that Beckert's name appears on it. They may have the file, but they do not have the man – one of the many substitutions in this film where written words, records, files and dossiers have taken on an independent life, replacing what they represent. The film shows the production of a gargantuan bureaucratic shadow reality. Archives upon archives are devoted to count, register and 'make up' people. The police organisation has already targeted Beckert as a possible suspect. His name is on a roster from which, in serial fashion, name after name is checked and eliminated as a suspect. Ironically, the police employ the same tactics of elimination by numbers as the serial killer does.

The film cuts from the list of former patients and present suspects to Beckert, as he leaves his house. Seconds later, Lohmann's assistant enters the frame; he studies his notebook where the name Hans Beckert is next on the list. The editing underscores the film's omniscient stance – the camera knows which of the many names on Lohmann's list is next. It shows us immediately the person whom we were led to believe is the murderer. There is a significant tension here: while the officials insist that the murderer is virtually indistinguishable and therefore undetectable, the film identifies and tracks the suspect from the beginning. We see Beckert accompanying the girl, we hear his compulsive whistling, we observe him as he observes himself in the mirror. Because of the ubiquitous camera, the anticipatory setup and the analytical editing, the spectators are regularly (with a few telling exceptions) a few steps ahead of the investigators. This permits the audience to adopt a detached, even amused, view of the proceedings and to throw critical light on the effectiveness of the investigation. The very structure of the film thus undermines the authority of the state: the audience knows more than the police.

In the wake of Lombroso and, in Germany, Erich Wulffen, it was not unusual to associate criminality with mental illness and to seek criminals among those who had been released from psychiatric hospitals. Beckert has already been marked – classified as a deviant – before he is branded with the letter 'M'. A telling scene may elucidate Beckert's psychiatric state. While Lohmann's assistant searches Beckert's room for clues, Beckert is in the street, involuntarily enacting his clinical history. The scene starts out with Beckert buying apples from a street vendor. The camera observes him in a long shot as he asks for another one. He then starts eating the fruit on the spot, a first sign of his compulsive need for instant gratification. He is attracted to a shop window display in a cutlery store with hundreds of knives, laid out in various geometrical shapes. An unusual medium shot of Beckert from inside the store window (actually from the perspective of the knives) produces a curious reflection in which rows of glistening knives frame his body and point at his heart. Marking in this way, if only for a few seconds, the knowledge that knives were Kürten's preferred instrument for killing, is a significant omen. The sheer mass of knives, slyly commenting at once on fashionably excessive consumption and on the submerged violence of Berlin's urban culture, seems to mesmerise Beckert. Suddenly, a young girl appears. She is multiply framed by this dazzling maze of windows, mirrors and reflections. She appears removed from him as if he were watching her on a movie screen. The vision triggers a visceral reaction. His body stiffens. The camera heightens the excitement and confusion with several cross-cuts, disorienting the viewer in this play of glances in which the knives become animated and almost seem to beckon Beckert to 'do it'. The camera returns to the girl. Beckert stands transfixed. He licks his lips and turns his head into profile, pushing his lips forward. The whistling begins, the outward sign that he is about to change Jekyll-and-Hyde-like into the 'other state' in which murders happen. Because of the store window's mirror effect, we see him doubled. Cut back to the girl. The space is empty. She must have left. Now he begins to stalk the girl. The camera closely follows him, unsteady, almost hand-held, in the style of today's stalker movies.

Another window display comes into view, one that is even more overtly symbolic than the cutlery shop. A phallic arrow bobs continuously up and down over a revolving spiral of concentric circles, evoking strong sexual associations. The same hypnotic spiral had appeared in Walter Ruttmann's 1927 documentary, *Berlin, Die Sinfonie der Großstadt* (Berlin, Symphony of a Big City) where it connoted an urban vertigo effect. Inspired by Marcel Duchamp's experiments with rotary glass plates and optical machines, the spiral was used as an advertising gimmick in 1920s window displays. In *M*, the manically moving objects correspond to Beckert's agitated state. His feral desire and lust radiate outward, animating all objects around him. Shot from his perspective, the girl passes

Window shopping

Beckert's desire …

… figured as violence

another enticing shop window; he and the camera follow her, then suddenly the girl's mother enters the frame and embraces her. A close call. The camera resumes its objective stance and shows him hiding in the shop entrance, clutching his heart, scratching his hand. Agitated and disorientated, he walks towards the camera and almost runs into it. Cut. A few minutes later he will be caught.

This street scene establishes a basis for Beckert's subsequent insanity plea before the kangaroo court. It also confirms his claim that he kills against his will. The scene's nexus of consumption and potential murder also links it to what Lang called the 'mass murder complex'. The girl is put on display, as if she herself was a commodity, a not-so-obscure object of desire, a fantasy, a movie. The sequence gestures towards a critique of a culture that consumes and is consumed by murder in fiction and in fact. The *mise-en-scène* of this passage revives the so-called street film, a genre of Weimar cinema that focused on the vicissitudes of urban modernity. It typically exposed a bourgeois man, driven by a strong desire for adventure, to the dangerous but alluring seductions of forbidden sexuality and criminality found in the nightly streets of the big city. In his review of Karl Grune's *Die Straße* (*The Street*, 1923), the prototype of the genre, Siegfried Kracauer wrote:

> The bustling of the characters imitates the movement of atoms: they do not meet, but rather bump up against each other, they pull apart without separating themselves. Instead of living connected to other things, they sink to the level of inanimate objects: automobiles, endless walls, the neon lights, which unburdened by time, flash on and off. Instead of filling space, they follow a path into the wasteland. Instead of communicating through language, they leave unsaid what might bring them together or pull them apart. Love is sex, murder is accident and tragedy never occurs. A wordless, soulless coexistence of directed automobiles and undirected desires ...[30]

Kracauer describes an urban environment which reduces people to inanimate objects – a hunting ground for the serial killer. The street is the site of unplanned possibilities and unknown dangers. 'The difficulty of solving this type of crime,' reasons Lohmann, 'is increased by the fact that the wrongdoer and the victim are only connected by a chance meeting. An instantaneous impulse is the killer's only motive.'

. . . .

Cut to the street with the blind balloon seller. We hear the whistling of the *Peer Gynt* tune off-screen. We see a shadow pass and recall the encounter between Beckert and Elsie Beckmann. The camera zooms in on the balloon seller, he seems to recognise the whistling and, like us, links it to the day of Elsie's murder. By the time he calls Heinrich, his assistant, to follow the suspect, however, the man has stopped whistling and is far away. (Heinrich must strain his eyes to see him.) Was it Beckert who whistled *Peer Gynt*? And was it his shadow? Lang begins to plant seeds of doubts. Heinrich runs off frame, while the balloon seller finishes his sentence. Lang heightens suspense by refusing to let the camera follow the action.

Will we miss something? Why not show us all? By the time Lang cuts to the pursuer, the man seems to have disappeared. Only a few agonising seconds later does Heinrich see him with a little girl inside a well-lit store for tropical fruit, strangely located below street level. Beckert emerges with the young girl, stops and puts a hand in his pocket. In an extreme close-up, we see his knuckles against the cloth of his pants as they reach into the pocket and pull out a switchblade. In another extreme close-up, the knife springs open and we glimpse the blade's blinding bright reflection. Will he use the weapon to kill the little girl? He takes the knife and – peels an orange. Lang plays a dark Hitchcockian game with the viewer's expectations; he demonstrates how easily images can deceive. Looking at the knife, the viewer anticipates a crime, possibly more graphic than the offscreen murder of Elsie. Heinrich observes this scene from a distance with growing apprehension (the camera shows him in several reaction shots, making him a stand-in viewer for us). To mark the murderer, he

Branding the suspect

spontaneously draws an 'M' on his palm with white chalk. He simply follows the outlines of creases that we all have in our palms. Pretending he has slipped on the orange peels, he slaps the letter on Beckert's shoulder. Frightened, Beckert drops the knife. In cruel irony, the girl picks it up and returns it to the murderer. The camera travels around him to show the gleaming white imprint against the dark coat. Beckert is unaware of it.

The suspected murderer is identified with the letter 'M' – a signifier with multiple possible meanings: *Mörder* (murderer), *Mensch* (human being), *Mutter* (mother), *Mann* (man), *Mabuse*, *Metropolis*. The sign condenses previous markings and stigmatises Beckert before our eyes. Marking is also a bureaucratic procedure for labelling and filing him alphabetically ('Murderer'), for cataloguing him as an 'M' in an archive from A to Z. To inscribe him in this way is to assign him a new identity that determines his subsequent actions. An anonymous 'Man without Qualities' (as Robert Musil called his 1930 novel) becomes trapped in a bureaucratic system that disciplines by labelling. Beckert, transformed into M, is now a moving target, designated for the kill.

As Beckert and the young girl continue their stroll, they walk by another shop window, again with a moving display: a jumping jack, opening and closing his legs in spastic motion as if to mimic the letter 'M'. Again the camera shoots the innocent child and a cherubic Beckert from inside the store, capturing their rapt smiles. When the child points out that he, the Man in Black (as the counting rhyme had it) picked up something white on his coat, he turns around, straining to see his back. He looks in a mirror next to the shop window, but suddenly starts. Staring at himself, his

Innocent and perverse rapture

The suspect caught by the camera

No escape

facial expression resembles the grimace he made in the earlier mirror scene. He looks straight into the camera, his eyes, showing the white around the pupils, wide open; he realises he is being observed. A marked man, he begins to run, with the hand-held camera in relentless pursuit.

. . . .

Muffled voices, screams of 'Let me go' from off-screen, a door is thrown open. Beckert, his jacket pulled over his head, is pushed down the stairs with brute force. He looks up, screaming, 'What do you want from me?' At the last two words, he turns around, his eyes widen in shock as he takes a step back. A reverse shot from his point of view reveals a gigantic assembly of criminals, crooks and prostitutes, filling a low cavernous hall to the rafters. They stare in complete silence. The film provides no explanation of these masses – they are simply there, a self-appointed court awaiting the defendant. For shock value, the camera had strictly assumed Beckert's viewpoint until it cuts to an extreme wide-angle shot, confronting us with the staggering mass of more than 200 representatives of the underworld. The camera begins to pan across a gallery of stone-faced (almost exclusively male) faces. Schränker and the other ringleaders sit at a table which is lit by a makeshift lamp in the shape of gallows. The eerie silence is broken by Beckert's yells: 'Help. Help. Let me go – get me out of here. Let me out.' To which Schränker coolly replies: 'You will not get out of here.' He addresses him in the familiar '*Du*' form, indicating from the start a contemptuous tone. The blind balloon seller, evoking Tiresias, the mythical blind seer, recognises the voice and identifies him. When he floats a balloon like Elsie Beckmann's, it triggers a violent flashback in Beckert. He utters 'Elsie, Elsie,' repeating Mrs Beckmann's distressed calls in the beginning of the film. This scene is shot from an extreme high angle, making the suspect look all the more vulnerable. When Schränker confronts him with photographs of missing children, Beckert recoils, approaching the camera with open hands, pleading that there must have been a mistake. The camera fastens on his face, so close to him as to be briefly out of focus, a reflection of his confusion about his place in this unnatural assembly.

The film treats the self-appointed jurors like an audience in a theatre, providing reaction shots while the action takes its course in real time. (Lorre is allowed to perform his monologue as if on stage.) The mock trial scene

The criminals' court

observes spatial and temporal unity for almost fifteen minutes – a striking contrast to the film's many brief scenes in different settings. Here Beckert finally gains a voice. Coming at the end of the film, his confession provides his own perspective and forces a re-evaluation of the entire story. The camera, which had been mobile and omniscient, implicating us in spying and surveying, comes to a halt and lets the suspect plead his case before a double audience: the jury in the movie and the spectators in the theatre.

The basic constellation of this scene – a man defends himself before a mock court – recalls Franz Kafka's *The Trial*, published in 1925 and widely discussed in Berlin at the time. Like Beckert, Joseph K. at first protests the legitimacy of his accusers, who make a mockery of the law. The court, characterised by the narrator as 'a crowd of the most varied sort', is criticised by K. for mishandling his case. He argues that the proceedings against him are 'only proceedings if I recognise them as such'. Kafka continues: 'K. interrupted himself and looked down into the hall. What he said was harsh, harsher than he had intended, but nonetheless accurate.'[31] Likewise, Beckert insults (perhaps also 'harsher than he had intended'?) his 'jurors' who sit in judgment over him: 'Who are you? All of you? Criminals! Perhaps you're even proud of yourselves? Proud of being able to break safes, to climb into buildings or cheat at cards . . .' Both K. and M are fully aware of the questionable legal status of their respective 'courts' and yet they fully submit to these bodies.

In *M*, the traditional narrative economy of a trial film (each character has a function and the relationship among them is predetermined) is undercut by constantly shifting roles: Beckert is both defendant and accuser, victim (driven insane by the 'voices' inside) and perpetrator, while Schränker, accused of three murders himself, acts as prosecutor. (During the break-in, he wore the uniform of a police officer.) The jury consists of ex-convicts, sarcastically introduced as 'experts in law'. Against this setting of crooks and thugs, the antiquated dignity of the elderly lawyer, played by the then well-known expressionist poet and performer Rudolf Blümner, seems incongruous and ironic. His belief in the written rule of law is dramatised by the presence of dusty old law books on his table. It is significant that no judge presides over this kangaroo court; this role is reserved for the movie audience.

There is a carnivalesque dimension to this 'court'. You do not climb up steps to a neoclassical courthouse; the court is held in the basement of a defunct cognac distillery. Lang also subverts the very

Prosecutor Schränker

Counsel for the Defence

purpose of the proceedings: 'court' and 'jurors' are not interested in truth or justice, but in the elimination of an outsider so that they can resume their illegal activities. The mockery of the law and its procedures is double-edged: it reflects cynicism of the Weimar judicial system, but, more importantly, it allows Lang to shift the parameter of the 'trial' from the question of truth and evidence to the question of retribution and the right to punish, from the letter of the law to the vagaries of justice. What is called into question here, according to Deleuze, is 'the very possibility of judging', because, for Lang, 'it is as if there is no truth any more, but only appearances'.[32] In fact, appearances themselves may tell the truth. Beckert, guilty or not, by his very confession demands that the law recognise him as a subject. Like later *film noir* heroes (such as Walter Neff in 1944's *Double Indemnity*), Beckert takes a perverse pleasure in the act of retelling his crimes. Although (or maybe, because) he knows that this court is a travesty, he seizes upon the chance to verbalise what long has been pent up. Since he is not there to be judged by the law (for he has not consciously committed a crime), it does not matter that this is no 'real' court. What does matter is that in this re-enactment he can constitute himself as a subject – finally to be heard and seen! He finds release in vocalising what has been repressed. If trials are public enactments of trauma, as Shoshana Felman has persuasively argued,[33] Beckert's 'trial' may point to a collective memory which refused to go away throughout the Weimar Republic: the shared trauma of wartime murder which deeply resonated among veterans and non-veterans alike.

. . . .

In his 1930 work journal, Lang recorded an idea for a scene in *M* that was never filmed: 'War scene as an excuse of the child murderer before the underworld court'.[34] If ever there was a doubt that World War I figured in Lang's mind as a subtext for *M*, this note dispels it. This scene might have been filmed as a flashback to Beckert's traumatic experience at the war front. It might have explained Beckert's drive to kill as a compulsion to repeat the murder that he was forced to commit in combat. Freud's work on war neurosis in 1918 sheds light on what the film leaves unsaid. The mental breakdowns of hundreds of thousands of soldiers, Freud argued, were the result of an unsolvable mental conflict that split the ego:

> The conflict is between the old ego of peacetime and the new war-ego of the soldier and it becomes acute as soon as the peace-ego is faced with the danger of being killed through the risky undertakings of his newly formed parasitical double. Or one might put it, the old ego protects itself from the danger to life by flight into the traumatic neurosis in defending itself against the new ego which it recognises as threatening its life.[35]

While the 'peace ego' does not want to kill, the 'war ego' must kill (or be killed) – Beckert's 'don't want to – must' is a doublebind conflict which, according to Freud, led to mental and somatic symptoms particularly among conscripted soldiers in the national army. What distinguished war neuroses from other traumatic neuroses was the threat of a coercive other voice that overwhelmed the old ego with the command to kill against one's will. Beckert expresses this precisely:

> I can't help myself! I haven't any control over this evil thing that's inside me – the fire, the voices, the torment ... It's there all the time, driving me out to wander through the streets ... following me ... Who knows what it's like to be me? How I'm forced to act ... How I must ... don't want to, must ... don't want to, must ...

Murder, for Beckert, thus becomes a *'passage à l'acte'* (Derrida), an act to resolve his inner conflict between the peace ego and the war ego.[36] He repeatedly restages the crime in order to reclaim the moment of the original trauma. What Beckert calls 'this evil thing that's inside me – the fire, the voices, the torment': these words are circumlocutions for forces that defy articulation. Because language has no words for his trauma, he resorts to the expressive power of his contorted hands and distorted facial features. His tortured body bears the full weight of the unsaid and the unsayable.

Why did Lang in the end not include a 'war scene'? There are several reasons. First, Lang was rightly afraid that to make the child murderer a war veteran may have turned the film into a war picture, a genre of no interest to him. Although the traumatic experience of the war front echoes throughout the film, culminating in Beckert's confession, Lang never mentions the war explicitly. Such a scene would also have provided a simple explanation and an excuse for Beckert's compulsion to kill. Most crucially, however, the scene might have put more emphasis on the origins of Beckert's condition than on its social consequences.

. . . .

The film represents Beckert as an outsider who is pathologised, doubly marked as clinically insane and criminal. He is the only one who speaks with a Southern dialect (the rest either speak heavy Berlin dialect or standard German), he looks stockier and rounder in body and face – features deemed out of keeping with the ideal of a tall 'Nordic' look, as embodied by Schränker/Gründgens. Schränker's long leather coat, bowler hat and black leather gloves, his eloquence and arrogant demeanour summon up images of a stylish Goebbels, chief Nazi orator and propagandist. Beckert, in contrast, wears a dark overcoat; he is the nursery rhyme's

Beckert's psychodrama

'Man in Black'. He lives by himself in a one-room sublet and stalks young girls. Even without the murders, he fits society's stereotypes about loners and perverts. Although the film does not dwell on his sexual deviance, the hints were clearly recognised by a culture saturated with images and narratives of *Lustmord*.[37] In addition, the classical serial murder cases of the 1920s, from Haarmann's cannibalism to Kürten's vampirism, had undertones of sexual perversion. But none of them killed only innocent children. Although the police poster also mentions a Kurt Klawitzky among the missing persons, little girls were the main victims. Lang magnified the heinousness of Beckert's crime by limiting it to the murder of children – considered (and confirmed by Dostoevsky's *The Brothers Karamazov*) to be the most horrifying of all crimes.

The nexus of sexual deviance and criminality carried anti-Semitic undertones, which did not have to be spelled out in 1931. Although Jack the Ripper, who killed exclusively prostitutes, was never found, the popular imagination of 1888 London identified him as an Eastern European Jew. Myths about sexual degeneracy linked Jews to prostitutes – both were outsiders and pariahs within Gentile society.[38] When Lang cast Peter Lorre (whose Hungarian name was Laszlo Loewenstein before he changed it to his stage name) as the child murderer, he could not have foreseen what the Nazis would do with his film. In 1940, a large portion of Beckert's confession scene was inserted in one of the most vicious anti-Semitic propaganda films, Fritz Hippler's documentary *Der ewige Jude* (The Eternal Jew). Identifying the actor with his role, the film claimed that the 'Jew Lorre' made the child murderer look like a sympathetic victim, thus subverting any sense of law and order. Beckert's body and his gait recalled the 'Operated Jew', found in Oskar Panizza's eponymous novella about anti-Semitic stereotypes. Beckert's un-German/un-Nordic penchant for *Südfrüchte* (imported fruit), as well as the implied nexus of sexual perversion, insanity and murder, readily connoted 'Jewishness' for those predisposed to anti-Semitic stereotypes in 1931. On the other hand, Schränker's declarations – 'This monster has no right to live … He must disappear. He must be exterminated, without pity, without scruples … this man should be snuffed out like a candle …' – strongly resembled Nazi rhetoric (soon to be put into practice by Hitler's euthanasia programs) for those who wanted to hear them as such. The roles Lorre and Gründgens played in *M* became inextricably bound to their life histories: Lorre, whose passport would have been marked with the sign 'J' had he remained in Germany, was forced to flee from the self-appointed mob executioners. Gründgens became one of the Reich's most celebrated theatre personalities.

Beckert is associated throughout the film with refuse – cigarette butts and pencil shavings (both of which establish his identity for the police) and discarded objects stored in the attic space of an office building. When he is discovered in this dark hiding place, he can hardly be distinguished from the clutter around him. He is a castaway and a misfit, but is he guilty of the murders committed? From a strictly legal point of view, Beckert is prosecuted for a crime for which there is no conclusive evidence. We never see him commit a crime, there are no witnesses, we do not even see a victim. While the film does show his uncontrollable inner urges, it shows no murders. The identification of a blind man based on a few whistled bars of a melody has nothing to do with the murder per se and the cigarette butts and pencil shavings are, at best, circumstantial evidence. The film thus invites us at least to entertain the possibility that Beckert might be one of those who wrote letters to the press claiming to be murderers (there were 200 such 'confessors' in the Kürten case), when in fact they were merely hankering for recognition, or fulfilling a desire for self-punishment. In his note, we see Beckert underline the word 'I' twice – like the letter, his confession is a self-affirmation, publicly performed and ecstatically acted out – self-incrimination as a psychotic break from life's seriality, from an outsider's expendability. On this level, it does not even matter if Beckert committed the murders or only imagined them. *M* for Lang was not a detective film or murder mystery (we know the suspect from the beginning), but rather a work that explored how a single misfit could tear an entire city's social fabric.

Beckert's unsolicited confession becomes a complex psychoanalytic session in which he works through his trauma before an audience torn between sympathy for his genuine pain (a few reaction shots show tough-looking men nodding in agreement and women clutching their handkerchiefs) and mistrust (is he really insane or just pretending?), between the spectacle of Beckert's theatrical performance and the practical matter at hand (his elimination, which is almost forgotten during his impassioned speech). Beckert's insanity plea recalls Georg Büchner's Woyzeck, the archetypal figure of the compulsive 'innocent murderer', who became part of Weimar's cultural memory following Alban Berg's modernist opera *Wozzeck* and its tumultuous premiere in Berlin in 1925.

The film can barely contain Beckert's rapturous act of self-fashioning; the confession's structural autonomy and oddity underscores the incompatibility of two orders in this scene, that of law (complicated by the fact that the state seems so impotent that the criminals must take the law into their own hands) and that of justice, which demands that the subject be delivered to a mental hospital. Beckert's confession suggests that he might be caught in the wrong film. His were not crimes the police or the underworld can prosecute and punish. Unable to help himself (as the whistling motif makes clear), he lives outside the law. What is a community to do with a subject whose very existence challenges the established order?

. . . .

On 12 May 1931, one day after *M*'s premiere, the League for Human Rights held a public debate about the death penalty. Using arguments from Lang's film to discuss the pending fate of Peter Kürten, the League's so-called abolitionists argued against the death penalty under any circumstances but met vociferous resistance.[39] The press reported the meeting as 'stormy'. While most citizens condemned the general public's 'instincts of revenge' and their 'desire for retribution', some saw Kürten's deliberate killings of two dozen people, his perverse sexuality and his manipulation of an hysterical public as exceptional and worthy of the death penalty. According to the reports of three psychiatrists, Kürten could not prove diminished mental capacity; therefore, Paragraph 51 of the Criminal Code did not apply. In contrast, Lang made sure that the audience was able to see that Beckert is not responsible for his crimes. The film seems to side with the lawyer who pleads for handing a sick person over to a mental asylum. The camera gives the lawyer centre stage, away from the rabble and above Beckert. Neither editing nor camera movement undercut his awkward nobility. One hand resting on his law books, the other dramatically gesticulating, he defies the verbal abuse from off-screen. The arguments of the underworld, however, accurately reflected the political and social climate of 1931: 'What happens if he breaks out of an asylum or gets released as cured?' Loud signs of approval accompany these rhetorical questions. Although Lang always insisted that *M* was a plea against the death penalty, the film is ambiguous enough that Goebbels could note in his diary of 21 May 1931: 'Fantastic! Against humanitarian sentimentality. For the death penalty. Well made. Lang will be our director one day.'[40]

And several journalists, ardent proponents of the abolition of the death penalty, were appalled by what they saw as Lang's ambivalent stance.

In the end, as the crowd becomes more agitated, the camera fixes upon the few women in the crowd. Gustave Le Bon (and, following him, Hitler in *Mein Kampf*) associated unruly masses with fickleness, gullibility and hysteria – traits which, in their minds, signified femininity. Lang, consciously or not, confirms this association when he shows a series of young prostitutes, one of whom savagely screams in close-up: 'Kill the beast.' The women heighten mass hysteria with references to motherhood and the loss of children. The camera augments the tension with a series of rapid close-ups of frenzied male faces that stare directly into the camera. When the lawyer demands that 'this human being be handed over to the police', a woman yells: 'This is *not* a human being!' – a process of literal dehumanisation that again resonates with the later Nazi slogans. After the lawyer pleads one last time that even a criminal deserves protection by the rule of law, the camera cuts in anticipation of the mob's action to an extreme long shot from above. The masses surge forward to kill Beckert – then stop dead in their tracks, immobile and silent. They slowly lift their arms, Schränker being the last to do so. In a shot that mirrors the first image of the trial scene, the camera records their reaction to an off-screen force. Unlike that first shot where the camera showed what Lorre saw, however, we see no countershot. We must assume a massive police presence, a higher force, a *deus ex machina*, that rescues Beckert from the lynch mob. Beckert raises himself from the fetal position he had assumed after his monologue. A disem-

The hand of the law

bodied hand reaches down to Beckert. Lohmann's voice, not anchored to a body, unlocalised and therefore omnipotent, announces: 'In the name of the law.'

Cut to a long shot of an empty courtroom. Judges clad in robes enter, one of them proclaims: 'In the name of the people.' The scene is brief and puzzling. It depicts no trial, no sentence, no defendant. The editing suggests that Beckert is the defendant, but we do not learn the verdict – a final confirmation that Lang did not care about the juridical outcome of his parable. Why then even bother to show the court? The film appears to legitimate the existence of a legal system as a higher authority than the mob's mock court; however, the restitution of legal authority is undercut, not only by the scene's extreme brevity, but also by its focus on the mere ritual of a court session. While the film acknowledges the legal system (and even its necessity, since Beckert is rescued from the lynch mob), it also challenges this institution's power and effectiveness. The camera (in a long shot) places the judges in the far distance. Their claim of speaking 'In the name of the people' is called into question by the subsequent scene which shows three women in mourning. One of them (Mrs Beckmann) declares with an expression of defiance and resignation: 'This [i.e. the court's decision, whatever it was] won't bring back our children either. We simply must keep a closer watch on our children.'

These laconic last words deflate any demonic notion of the serial killer, who, on the contrary, is shown finally as pitiful and unremarkable, neither in command of his drives nor of his obese body. The mother's message suggests that even after this particular serial killer is dispatched, new ones will follow. The words also betray the public lack of trust in the state's power to protect its citizens. When Mrs Beckmann declares that we must watch out for our children, the 1931 version (according to the censorship records) added the imperative: 'You, too, you, too', a direct address to the audience which 'rhymes' with the first words in the film that threaten with the Man in Black coming to you, too.

The exhortative words 'You, too!' served as the final phrase of a lengthy article by Thea von Harbou, entitled 'Why exactly "such" a film?' published in the *Berliner Volkszeitung* on 12 May 1931. This piece considers *M* less from the perspective of the criminal and the pursuit of him by police and gangsters (an entirely male affair) than from the perspective of the female victims who have hardly a voice in the film: the mothers and the children. She argues that not enough is done to protect children from violence in the streets and asks in a tone appropriate to the leftist liberal paper in which the article appeared: 'How is a woman who has to go to work in the factories and offices supposed to ensure a safe life for her children?' She insists that everyone should feel more responsible for the community, that public sentiments should become more attuned to the needs of those people whose children are endangered. *M* was meant to alert the audience and to exhort people to protect their children, in Harbou's mind a mission that was as important as the fight against unemployment and homelessness: 'This film ... shows how little it takes for a tragedy of a child – a tragedy of a mother – to occur and how easily this could happen again any day. Nobody has the right to respond indifferently and to say: What do I care?! Everyone is called upon. Everyone is responsible. You too.'

The film's final scene shows three women in a tightly framed tableau shot which provides both a coda and a return to the film's beginning with its emphasis on children and mothers. Mrs Beckmann joins two other grieving women in a highly sculptural triad reminiscent of the three Sisters of Fate (Parcae in Roman mythology, Moirae in Greek and Nornes in Norse) who regulate man's destiny. This visual reference to fate and destiny dramatises a larger tension at work in the film, the tension between the forces of modernity with their emphasis on time, discipline, rationality, seriality, law and order, and those recalcitrant counterforces – trauma, passion, illness, loss and, finally, death – that defy reason and resist integration. *M* explores this tension, but offers no solution beyond a distraught mother's call for vigilance.

Three Sisters of Fate

5

....

LOS ANGELES, 1951

Same title, different film. Joseph Losey's *M*, a *film noir* remake of Lang's *M*, opened in New York on 11 June 1951, almost twenty years after the original caused such a stir in Berlin. Losey's film follows the same storyline, but is set in Los Angeles; it centres on the same conflicts, but updates them for postwar American audiences. Although Fritz Lang and several of the original cast, including Peter Lorre, lived in Hollywood, none of them participated in the production. The remake was the idea of Seymour Nebenzal (formerly Nebenzahl), the producer of the original *M*. Along with many others from the German film industry, Nebenzal had fled the Nazis before he was marked – not with an 'M' in chalk, but with a yellow star.

Nebenzal wanted Lang to remake his most successful film, but Lang flatly refused. *M* was a 'classic', he said, 'it is stupid to try to improve on it.'[41] Nebenzal reports that Lang was opposed 'because there is no organised group of beggars in the United States, therefore the premise of the original film is not valid here.' Astonished, Nebenzal countered: 'I always thought and still think, that the problems connected with a sex criminal of this type, his menace to the community and the treatment of such criminals was the basic premise of the story – a problem which is much more acute today in the United States than the few isolated cases were in Germany in the early 1930s.' In addition, he claimed: 'The German picture was never generally released in the United States, but was shown only in some art houses and by the Museum of Modern Art. Only a very small percentage of theatregoers have seen it – and they had to depend on subtitles.' Nebenzal's account is not quite accurate. According to the *New York Times* of 3 April 1933, Lang's *M* did open in New York in a subtitled version, but played only for a week before a British-produced dubbed version ran with slightly more success. Joseph Losey, an American theatre and film director, had close ties to the German exile community in Los Angeles. In 1947, he directed the highly praised stage production of Brecht's *Galileo Galilei* with Charles Laughton; he also made several *film noirs* before Nebenzal called on him in 1950 to remake *M*. Because of earlier Communist sympathies, he was under active surveillance by the House Un-American Activity Committee (HUAC), which began its witch-hunt against 'Red Hollywood' in October 1947. Losey had a hard time finding a film script that would pass the Censorship Office; a remake of a classic had better chances of being approved. He was reluctant at first, as he admitted, because Lang's *M* 'is and remains a classic, which one doesn't want to compete with',[42] but he wanted to work and, in addition, he had found an actor, David Wayne, whom he considered to be perfect for Lorre's part.

Wayne, a stage actor, played the child murderer as a nervous man, possessed from the beginning by a curious shoe fetish and a clinical desire to be punished for childhood misdeeds. There is more Freud in the Hollywood remake than in Lang's original! Wayne, lean and lanky, looks more like Anthony Perkins in *Psycho* than the plumpish Lorre. There are other changes that make Losey's *M* a remake in name only. The people of Los Angeles no longer read newspapers, they watch television. The organisation of the beggars becomes a fleet of taxi drivers – a change that allowed Losey's camera to explore the streets of Los Angeles. Unlike Lang's *M*, this film is almost exclusively shot on location, capturing an old, European-looking Los Angeles that in the meantime has disappeared as a result of urban redevelopment. If overhead shots were the predominant camera position in Lang's *M*, the camera of the remake is mobile, often shooting through window shields of moving taxis. Lang's claustro-

phobic and implosive space is now fluid and decentralised, but, despite its dispersion, it is no less dangerous. Losey's remake fleshes out Lang's modernist abstractions: it makes the story into a psycho-thriller with realistic characters, set in a recognisable Los Angeles milieu.

M's shadow falls over a large number of *film noirs*. One of the reasons why Lang may have opposed a remake is that most of his own work in Hollywood could be called, with only slight exaggeration, one grand reworking of *M* –

not merely in reusing its visual and narrative tropes, but more importantly in responding to questions that the film of 1931 had left unresolved. Lang's first film made in the United States, *Fury* (1936), deals more thoroughly than *M* with the emergence of a lynch mob; it also poses the question of punishment for the instigators of a manhunt. His last two Hollywood films, *While the City Sleeps* and *Beyond a Reasonable Doubt* (both 1956), deal with murder and the problematic interaction of press and police. *The Blue Gardenia* (1953) revisits a society addicted to murder mysteries. In this film, we also meet self-incriminators who implicate themselves in a murder investigation. The underlying ideas of Lang's American films (the nexus of crime, mass culture and urban modernity; the fate of innocent people fighting omnipotent external forces or uncontrollable, self-destructive urges; the tension between justice and law) were already at the heart of *M*. Lang's use of space and light and his famous mise-en-scène inspired many filmmakers in their constructions of a noir universe. *M*'s play of shadows, low-key and high-contrast lighting, extreme camera angles and its emphasis on compositional tension rather than physical action, lived on in many *film noirs* of the 1940s and 1950s. The spaces of *noir* are, as in *M*, empty office buildings and warehouses, city streets, claustrophobic pubs or cluttered detective offices. When *M* was first shown in New York in 1933, it appeared as the antithesis to recent American gangster films such as *Little Caesar* (1930) and *Scarface* (1932). *M* did not share the gangster film's dream of upward mobility, its moral certitude and its love of violent action. 'It is a picture,' the film critic of the *New Republic* remarked, 'which I do not believe could under any circumstances have been made in Hollywood – indeed, any American director who suggested such a thing would probably find his own sanity suspected. Nevertheless, Hollywood will make better pictures seeing this one.'[43]

In Hollywood exile, Lorre repeatedly played his role as the strange but pitiful murderer, beginning with the aptly entitled *The Stranger on the Third Floor* (1940). 'Lorre became the first actor to put a sad, scary – and human – face on crime,' a recent popular guide to *film noir* declares. 'This was essential to the development of *noir* and *M* deserves to be recognised among the genre's earliest progenitors.'[44]

Returning to Germany in 1951, Lorre wrote, directed and starred in his own film, *Der Verlorene* (The Lost One, 1951). It is the story (told in flashbacks) of a scientist, who, working for the Nazis, turns into a compulsive serial killer, mimicking on a small scale the state-sanctioned mass murder. Because his crimes have been covered up by the state that needs his services, he can find justice only by throwing himself under a train. The film is shot in stark chiaroscuro, offering an uncompromisingly bleak picture of a deeply traumatised, world-weary man who suffers from a repetition compulsion and cannot stop killing after his first murder – in a faint echo of Lorre's sensational debut role in Lang's *M* twenty years before. The hopes Lorre pinned on his directorial accomplishment came to naught. *The Lost One* was a complete flop in a postwar Germany that did not want to be reminded of its past. Lorre returned to Hollywood where his roles sadly declined to the point of self-parody.

Los Angeles, 1951. Ethel and Julius Rosenberg are found guilty of treason and sentenced to death – for many, the trial confirmed the danger of Communist subversion, for many others it offered a terrifying miscarriage of justice. Capitalising on the nation's fear of Communist aggression, J. Edgar Hoover warned of Soviet infiltration. Joseph McCarthy widened his investigation of red sympathisers to include scientists, diplomats, academics and all of Hollywood. An atmosphere of suspiciousness weighed heavily on the nation – anyone could be targeted and marked as a suspect.

Losey's remake was as topical in 1951 as Lang's *M* was in 1931. It was not hard to see it as a commentary, only thinly veiled, on HUAC's destruction of careers and livelihoods, often through mere insinuation and innuendo. Losey enlarged the role of the lawyer as the voice of law and reason, calling him Langley (a blend of Lang and Losey). Flawed because of a serious drinking problem, but upright and uncompromising, he becomes the spokesman for the film's political message. As he stands up against mob mentality, he is shot. At the end of the film, he lies dead on the ground. The camera holds this shot as if to memorialise him as an innocent victim of inhuman manhunts, no matter where.

APPENDIX: THE MISSING SCENE

....

What follows is a literal translation of a missing scene from Lang's *M* as it was submitted to the Censorship Board in Berlin on 27 April 1931, two weeks before the opening. This board required a copy of the film and the so-called *Zensurkarten* (censorship cards), which contained a written record of all spoken dialogue and textual material. Although they do not indicate details about staging or camera movement, or even the names of the speakers, they have been invaluable in reconstructing early films in their original sequence of scenes. In the case of Lang's *M*, the approved version was recorded as being 3208 metres long, with a running time of 117 minutes. The most complete version we presently own falls six minutes short. Because *M*'s censorship cards have recently surfaced, we have a record of one scene that is either missing from the extant print (i.e. it could still turn up one day) or lost (i.e. it was cut by Lang after the premiere). The scene deals with the baffling phenomenon of self-incrimination by citizens who are eager to become part of the media madness (as happened in the case of Kürten). A review of *M*'s opening in *Film-Journal* (17 May 1931) mentions the film's critique of the 'self-incrimination of innocent people' and allows us to conclude that the premiere version of 11 May 1931 still contained this scene.

The missing sequence, reprinted below for the first time, originally followed the scene in which a mob-like crowd attacks a pickpocket, thinking it has caught the child murderer. The sequence begins with a police poster reporting the murder of Elsie Beckmann and showing the increased reward. The scene then cuts to a group of citizens all claiming to be the murderer. As the production still below shows, they gleefully write letters and cut out type from a newspaper to conceal their handwriting. (The unpublished photograph was found in the Horst von Harbou collection of production stills from *M*.) Cut to the office of Inspector Lohmann who is busy placing a phone call while dictating a press release about those 'most effective allies of the

Self-incriminators at work

police', the press and public. This pronouncement is soon ironically undercut by subsequent phone calls from self-incriminators hampering the investigation and by journalists eager to whip up mass hysteria. Lohmann appears to carry on two conversations simultaneously: one with a citizen from Dresden (speaking, according to the script, in untranslatable, comical Saxon dialect), who insists that he is the serial killer; another with the editor-in-chief of a newspaper who wants to know what progress has been made. When Lohmann realizes that the would-be murderer from Dresden simply wants his name in the paper and a free trip to Berlin, he cuts him off. To the newspaper editor he complains, increasingly irritated, that his investigation is most occupied in dealing with self-incriminators. At this point the missing scene concludes; it is followed by a close-up of the headline: 'Murderer Writes to the Press'. In the absence of this sequence, the present version of *M* cuts abruptly from the mob scene mentioned above to the newspaper banner.

47. 15,000 Mark Reward! Another Child Murder. Elsie Beckmann, eight years old, having resided with her mother at Marienstraße 519/IV, was found dead with heavy wounds today around 2 p.m. in a bush at the Wohlitzer Chaussee, close to Kilometre Mark 7,3.

48. I am the murderer! It was me! I did it! I am the murderer! I did it! I am the murderer! I did it!

49. Damn it. Damn. Miss. Dönhoff 3600. [A Berlin phone number; A.K.]

50. Press and public. Press and public … Do you have it down, Miss?

51. Yes.

52. Are … are the most effective allies of the police.

53. Yes? Yes … Just a moment … self-incrimination of the child murderer.

54. Oh no! Hello, yes … how … but, for Christ's sake, don't be so nervous. So … well … that's now already the third one who claims to have done it. One in Hamburg, one in Dresden and … Who? … Oh well, fine, do go there, maybe it's him after all. What now?

55. The photographic plates the police want to have printed in the second evening edition.

56. Okay, fine, off you go. What do you want?

57. What headline?

58. Okay … well … say this: He is in our midst.

59. He is in our midst. Thank you.

60. Connection with telephone office Dresden, Police Department.

61. Man, don't babble. I know exactly who you are. You suffer from megalomania. A while ago, you also wanted to be the one who broke into the bank on Kleist Street.

62. But, Inspector, I should know best whether I did it. I don't mind coming personally to …

63. Yes, I believe it. To come to Berlin on state funds, right? You'd like that, right? … Yes … Unfortunately no, Mr Chief Editor … it's one of the usual self-incriminations.… (off he goes) … No … No … No … Yes … Yes … Yes … Yes … Of course … Yes … Yes. These people make me puke.… but no idea! Please … please … yes. Good evening.

64. Well, will I now get into the papers after all, Inspector?

65. Yes, into the funny papers.

66. The *Berliner Abendzeitung*, Inspector.

67. Oh well. That will get us into trouble again.

68. Headline in *Tempo*: 'Murderer Writes to the Press'.

69. Letter as in title 28, roll 1. [*Because the Police did not pass on my first letter to the public, I am now turning directly to the press. Investigate and you will find everything confirmed. But I am not through yet.*]

NOTES

· ·

Full references, where not supplied, can be found in the bibliography.

1 Fritz Lang, 'Mein Film *M*': Ein Tatsachenbericht', *Die Filmwoche*, vol. 9, 20 May 1931.

2 Quotations from the film follow the subtitles of the restored version (VHS Janus Films/Home Vision Cinema MMM 010), but are occasionally modified to correspond more closely to the German dialogue.

3 See Michel Chion, *The Voice in Cinema*, trans. by Claudia Gorbman (New York: Columbia University Press, 1999).

4 Fritz Lang, Arbeitsjournal 1930 (unpublished). Publication by permission of the Stiftung Deutsche Kinemathek Berlin.

5 D. A. Miller, *The Novel and the Police* (Berkeley: University of California Press, 1988), p. 23.

6 'Fritz Lang wieder film-aktiv', *Film-Kurier*, 6 June 1930.

7 'Hitler's Zeugen-Aussage in Moabit', *Vossische Zeitung*, 9 May 1931.

8 'Fritz Lang Film ohne Titel', *Film-Kurier*, 20 April 1930. Both Robert Siodmak's *The Man Who Searches for His Murderer* and Fedor Ozep's *The Murderer Dimitri Karamasoff* appeared in 1931.

9 O. A. Palitzsch, 'Broadcast Literature', in Kaes, Jay & Dimendberg, *The Weimar Republic Sourcebook*, p. 600.

10 Lang, 'Die mimische Kunst im Lichtspiel', in Gehler & Kasten, *Fritz Lang*, p. 256f.

11 'Würden Sie noch einen Stummfilm drehen?', *Film-Kurier*, 1 July 1930.

12 Carroll, 'Lang, Pabst, and Sound', p. 266.

13 See Jeanpaul Goergen, *Walter Ruttmanns Tonmontagen als Ars Acustica* (Siegen: MuK, 1994).

14 Lang, in *M. Protokoll*, p. 126.

15 Ibid., p. 125.

16 Kurt Pinthus, 'Marieluise Fleisser, Pioniere in Ingolstadt', *8-Uhr-Abendblatt*, 2 April 1929.

17 Lenk, *Peter Kürten*, p. 257.

18 On the contemporary American scene, see Mark Seltzer, *Serial Killers: Death and Life in America's Wound Culture* (New York: Routledge, 1998).

19 I thank Sara Hall for the reference to this source.

20 See, for instance, Gabriele Tergit, 'Fritz Lang's *M*: Filmed Sadism', in Kaes, Jay & Dimendberg, *The Weimar Republic Sourcebook*, pp. 632–4.

21 Lang, 'Mein Film *M*' (see footnote 1).

22 Ernst Gennat, 'Die Düsseldorfer Sexualverbrechen', *Kriminalistische Monatshefte*, vol. 4 (April 1930), pp. 80–1.

23 On the philosophical concept of seriality, see Jean-Paul Sartre, *Critique of Dialectical Reason*, vol. 1, trans. Alan Sheridan-Smith (London: New Left Books, 1976), pp. 253–76, 642–54; also Benedict Anderson, 'Nationalism, Identity and the Logic of Seriality', in *The Spectre of Comparisons: Nationalism, Southeast Asia and the World* (London: Verso, 1998), pp. 29–45.

24 Lessing, in *Monsters of Weimar*, p. 19f. (Subsequent page numbers refer to this edition.)

25 More recent films include Uli Lommel's *Die Zärtlichkeit der Wölfe* (1973, with Kurt Raab & R. W. Fassbinder) and Romuald Karmaka's *Der Totmacher* (1995).

26 Ernst Jünger, 'Total Mobilization', in Richard Wolin (ed), *The Heidegger Controversy: A Critical Reader* (New York: Columbia University Press, 1991), pp. 119–39.

27 Lang is fond of irregularities, imperfections and contingencies that disturb any dream of total control. For instance, the fingerprint sample for the right hand of a criminal, suitably nicknamed 'Four-Finger-Ernst', misses one finger. One box on the chart is blank. Another example: when Lohmann reads a neatly typed police report, he discovers and corrects a common misspelling, crossing out an 'e' and calling the author 'idiot'. Human error occurs on the level of a single letter – not insignificant in a film whose title is 'M'.

28 Michel Foucault, *Discipline and Punish: the Birth of the Prison*, trans. Alan Sheridan (New York: Vintage, 1979), p. 187.

29 Fritz Lang, 'Das Gesicht des Mörders,' *Tempo*, 11 May 1931.

30 Siegfried Kracauer, 'Die Straße', *Frankfurter Zeitung*, 3 February 1924.

31 Franz Kafka, *The Trial*, trans. Breon Mitchell (New York: Schocken, 1998), p. 45.

32 Gilles Deleuze, *Cinema 2. The Time-Image*, trans. Hugh Tomlinson and Robert Gatetor (Minneapolis: University of Minnesota Press, 1989), p. 138.

33 Shoshana Felman, 'Forms of Judicial Blindness, or the Evidence of What cannot be Seen', *Critical Inquiry*, vol. 23 (Summer 1997), pp. 738–88.

34 See note 3.

35 Sigmund Freud, Introduction to *Psycho-Analysis and the War Neuroses* (London: International Psycho-Analytical Press, 1921), p. 3.

36 On this concept, see Renata Salecl, 'Crime as a Mode of Subjectivization: Lacan and the Law', *Law and Critique*, vol. 4, 1993, pp. 3–20.

37 See Tatar, *Lustmord*.

38 See Sander L. Gilman, 'The Jewish Murderer', in *The Jew's Body* (New York & London: Routledge, 1991), pp. 104–27.

39 On the question of *M* and the death penalty, see Evans, *Rituals of Retribution*, pp. 596–605; and Jankowski, *Warte, warte … On the contemporaneous debates*, see E. M. Mungenast, *Der Mörder und der Staat* (Stuttgart: Hädecke Verlag, 1928); Franz Alexander and Hugo Staub, *The Criminal, the Judge and the Public* (Glencoe, Illinois: The Free Press, 1929).

40 Ralf Georg Reuth (ed.), *Joseph Goebbels Tagebücher 1924-1945* (Munich: Piper, 1992), vol. 2, p. 68.

41 Quoted in Dimendberg, 'From Berlin to Bunker Hill', p. 86. Nebenzal's subsequent quotations also from Dimendberg, p. 86. See also Thomas Elsaesser who reports that Lang 'was not prepared to acknowledge the director [Losey] as a member of his profession'. 'Joseph Losey: Time Lost and Found', *Monthly Film Bulletin*, June 1985, p. 173. See further David Caute, *Joseph Losey: A Revenge on Life* (New York: Oxford University Press, 1994), pp. 92–96.

42 Dimendberg, 'From Berlin to Bunker Hill', p. 78.

43 B. B., 'Four Films: Art and propaganda', *The New Republic*, 19 April 1933, p. 283.

44 Eddie Muller, *Dark City: The Lost World of Film Noir* (New York: St Martin's Press, 1998), p. 111.

Publisher's Note:

M is available on BFI Video, in its fully restored original version, digitally remastered. Cat No. BFIV 024, £12.99.

CREDITS

· ·

M

Germany
1931
German Release
11 May 1931
Distributor
Vereinigte Star-Film GmbH
British Release
June 1932 (8818 feet)
British Distributor
National Distributors

Production Company
Nero-Film AG, Berlin
Producer
Seymour Nebenzahl
**Unit Production
Manager**
Gustav Rathje
Director
Fritz Lang
Screenplay
Thea von Harbou, Fritz
Lang
**Supervising
Photographer**
Fritz Arno Wagner
Camera
Fritz Arno Wagner
Karl Vaß
Stills
Horst von Harbou
Editor
Paul Falkenberg
Art Director
Emil Hasler
Set Decorators
Emil Hasler, Karl Vollbrecht
Music
Theme from 'Peer Gynt' by
Edvard Grieg, whistled by
Fritz Lang
Sound
Adolf Jansen

Cast
Peter Lorre
Hans Beckert
Ellen Widmann
Frau Beckmann, the mother
Inge Landgut
Elsie Beckmann, the child

Gustaf Gründgens
Schränker
Friedrich Gnaß
burglar
Fritz Odemar
cardsharp
Paul Kemp
pickpocket
Theo Lingen
confidence man
Ernst Stahl-Nachbaur
chief of police
Franz Stein
minister
Otto Wernicke
Police Inspector Lohmann
Theodor Loos
Police Inspector Groeber
Georg John
blind streethawker
Rudolf Blümner
defence counsel
Karl Platen
nightwatchman
Gerhard Bienert
police inspector's secretary
Rosa Valetti
barmaid of the Crocodile
Club
Hertha von Walther
prostitute
Josef Almas
Carl Balhaus
Hans Behal
Josef Dahmen
Hugo Döblin
J.A Eckhoff
Else Ehser
Karl Elzer
Erwin Faber
Dr. Erich Frey
Ilse Fürstenberg
Heinrich Gotho
Heinrich Gretler
Günther Hadank
Robert Hartberg
Ernst Paul Hempel
Oskar Höcker
Albert Hörrmann
Albert Karchow
Werner Kepich

Hermann Krehan
Rose Lichtenstein
Lotte Loebinger
Sigurd Lohde
Alfred Loretto
Paul Mederow
Margarete Melzer
Trude Moos
Hadrian Maria Netto
Maja Norden
Edgar Pauly
Klaus Pohl
Franz Pollandt
Paul Rehkopf
Hans Ritter
Max Sablotzki
Alexander Sascha
Leonard Steckel
Karl Heinz Stroux
Wolf Trutz
Otto Waldis
Borwin Walth
Rolf Wanka
Ernst Wulf
Bruno Ziener
and
Carell
Gelingk
Goldstein
Anna Goltz
Isenta
Kurth
Leeser
Maschek
Matthis
Günther Neumann
Nied
Rebane
Reihsig
Rhaden
**Agnes Schulz-
Lichterfeld**
Swinborne
Wannemann

Black and White
10,525 feet
117 minutes

Credits compiled by BFI
Filmographic Unit

BIBLIOGRAPHY

·························

Bellour, Raymond, 'On Fritz Lang', in Stephen Jenkins (ed.) *Fritz Lang: The Image and the Look* (London: BFI, 1981), pp. 26–37.

Bogdanovich, Peter, 'Fritz Lang', in *Who the Devil Made It* (New York: Knopf, 1997), pp. 170–234.

Burch, Noel, 'Fritz Lang: German Period', in Richard Roud (ed.) *Cinema: A Critical Dictionary*, vol. 2 (London: Secker & Warburg, 1980), pp. 583–99.

——, & Jorge Dana, 'Propositions', *Afterimage*, vol. 5 (Spring 1974), pp. 40–66.

Carroll, Noel, 'Lang, Pabst and Sound', *Cine-Tracts*, vol. 2 no. 1, Fall 1978, pp. 15–23.

Chang, Joseph S. M. J., '*M*: A reconsideration', *Literature/Film Quarterly*, vol. 7 no. 4, 1979, pp. 300–8.

Dadoun, Roger, 'Le pouvoir et "sa" folie', *Positif*, 188, December 1976, pp. 13–20.

Del Ministro, Maurizio, 'Una ipotesi psicoanalitica per la lettura di *M*', *Cinema Nuovo*, vol. 16 no. 250, November–December 1977, pp. 451–4.

DeNitto, Dennis & William Herman, *Film and the Critical Eye* (New York: Macmillan, 1975), pp. 104–36.

Dimendberg, Edward, 'From Berlin to Bunker Hill: Urban Space, Late Modernity, and Film Noir in Fritz Lang's and Joseph Losey's *M*', *Wide Angle*, vol. 19, October 1997, pp. 62–93.

'Dossier: Fritz Lang', *Positif*, vol. 365, July/August 1991, pp. 124–60.

Douchet, Jean, et al. (German adaptation by Frieda Grafe and Enno Patalas) *M von Fritz Lang* (Video Institut für Film und Bild/Cinémathèque Française, 1989)

Dütsch, Werner, 'Fritz Lang: Ein Essay', *Steadycam*, no. 18, 1991, pp. 29–49.

Eisenschitz, Bernard & Paolo Bertetto (eds), *Fritz Lang: La mise en scène* (Torino: Lindau, n.d.).

Eisner, Lotte H., *Fritz Lang* (New York: Oxford University Press, 1977).

——, 'Le Style de *M le Maudit*', *L'Avant-Scène du Cinéma*, no. 39, July–August 1964, pp. 5–6.

Evans, Richard J., *Rituals of Retribution: Capital Punishment in Germany, 1600–1986* (Oxford: Oxford University Press, 1996).

Fabe, Marilyn, *M – Searching for a Victim: Notes and Analysis*, Film Study Extract (Mount Vernon: Macmillan Films, Inc., 1976).

Färber, Helmut, 'Drei Fotografien von den Dreharbeiten zu *M* von Fritz Lang', in Uta Berg-Ganschow and Wolfgang Jacobsen (eds), ... *Film ... Stadt ... Kino ... Berlin* (Berlin: Argon, 1987), pp. 113-16.

Farocki, Harun, *Peter Lorre – Das doppelte Gesicht* (Video West 3, 1985).

Ferro, Marc, '"The Fait Divers" and the Writing of History in Fritz Lang's *M*', in *Cinema and History*, trans. Naomi Greene (Detroit: Wayne State University Press, 1988), pp. 154–7.

Garncarz, Joseph, 'Fritz Lang's *M*: A Case of Significant Film Variation', *Film History*, vol. 4 no. 3, 1990, pp. 219–26.

Garnham, Nicholas, *M: A Film by Fritz Lang* (New York: Simon & Schuster Classic Film Scripts, 1968).

——, 'Reply to Thierry Kuntzel's "The Treatment of Ideology in the Textual Analysis of Film"', *Screen*, vol. 14 no. 3, Autumn 1973, pp. 55–8.

Gehler, Fred & Ullrich Kasten, *Fritz Lang, die Stimme von Metropolis* (Berlin: Henschel Verlag, 1990).

Goethe Institute Nancy (ed.), 'Fritz Lang's *M*', in *Sequenz 1: Film und Pädagogik* (1986).

Grafe, Frieda, 'Für Fritz Lang', in *Fritz Lang* (Munich: Hanser, 1976), pp. 7–82.

Hall, Sara F., 'Tracing the Transgressor: Professional Criminology and Amateur Detection in Weimar Republic Mass Media', in *Vagabondage: The Poetics and Politics of Movement* (Berkeley: Berkeley Academic Press, 1997).

Hoffheimer, Michael H., 'Artistic Convention and Natural Law. Didactic Treatment of Justic and Authority in Works of Fielding, Hawthorne, and Fritz Lang', *Temple Law Review*, vol. 63 no. 3, 1990, pp. 483–509.

Hofmann, Felix & Stephen D. Youngkin, *Peter Lorre* (Munich: Belleville, 1998).

Jahnke, Eckart, 'Fritz Lang's *M*', *Filmwissenschaftliche Mitteilungen*, vol. 6 (1965), pp. 169–206.

Jankowski, Stephan, *Warte, warte nur ein Weilchen ... Die Diskussion um die Todesstrafe in Fritz Langs Film 'M'* (Wetzlar: Edition Kletzmeier, 1998).

Jenkins, Stephen (ed.), *Fritz Lang: The Image and the Look* (London: BFI, 1981).

Kaes, Anton, 'The Cold Gaze: Notes on Mobilization and Modernity', *New German Critique*, vol. 59, Spring/Summer 1993, pp. 105–17.

——, Martin Jay & Edward Dimendberg (eds), *The Weimar Republic Sourcebook* (Berkeley: University of California Press, 1994).

Kaplan, E. Ann, *Fritz Lang: A Guide to References and Resources* (Boston: G. K. Hall, 1981).

Keusch, Donat, 'Zur Tonrestaurierung von *M*', *Filmgeschichte*, vol. 7/8 (June 1996), pp. 38–9.

Kinder, Marsha & Beverly Houston, *Close-up: A Critical Perspective* (New York: Harcourt, Brace, Jovanovich, 1972), pp. 56–66.

Kracauer, Siegfried, 'Murderers Among Us', in *From Caligari to Hitler: A Psychological History of the German Film* (Princeton: Princeton University Press, 1947), pp. 218–22.

Kreimeier, Klaus, 'Strukturen im Chaos: Wie Fritz Lang Ordnung in den Dschungel bringt', in Irmbert Schenk (ed.), *Dschungel Großstadt: Kino und Modernisierung* (Marburg: Schüren, 1999), pp. 57–66.

Kuntzel, Thierry, 'Le Travail du Film', *Communication*, no. 19 (reprinted as 'The film work', *Enclitic*, vol. 2 no. 1, Spring 1978, pp. 39–64).

——, 'The Treatment of Ideology in the Textual Analysis of Film', *Screen*, vol. 14 no. 3, Autumn 1973, pp. 44–54.

Lenk, Elisabeth & Katharina Kaever (eds), *Peter Kürten, genannt der Vampir von Düsseldorf* (Frankfurt a.M.: Eichborn, 1997).

Lessing, Theodor, 'Haarmann: The Story of a Werewolf', in *Monsters of Weimar* (London: Nemesis Books, 1993), pp. 11–156.

Lefèvre, Raymond, '*M le Maudit*', *Image et son*, vol. 152 (June 1962), pp. 17–23.

Linder, Joachim, 'Fahnder und Verbrecher in Fritz Langs deutschen Polizeifilmen', *Spiel* (1999), pp. 181–215.

'*M*', in *Masterworks of the German Cinema* (New York: Harper & Row, 1973), pp. 97–177.

'*M le Maudit*', *L'avant-Scène du Cinéma*, no. 39, July–August 1964, pp. 7–41.

M. Protokoll: Mit einem Interview des Regisseurs von Gero Gandert (Hamburg: Marion von Schröder Verlag, 1963).

McGilligan, Patrick, *Fritz Lang: The Nature of the Beast* (New York: St Martin's Press, 1997).

McKenna, Andrew, 'Pubic Execution', in John Denver (ed.), *Legal Reelism: Movies as Legal Texts* (Urbana: University of Illinois Press, 1996), pp. 225–43.

Marie, Michel, M le Maudit:*étude critique* (Paris: Nathan, 1989).

Mesnil, Michel, *Fritz Lang: le jugement* (Paris: Editions Michalon, 1966).

Monsters of Weimar (London: Nemesis Books, 1993).

Palao, José Antonio, 'El demonio en el laberinto. Una lectura de *M*', in Vicente Sanchez-Biosca (ed.) *Más allá de la duda. El cine de Fritz Lang* (Valencia: Universitat de Valencia, 1992), pp. 67–75.

Patalas, Enno, 'Der Fall *M*'. *Filmgeschichte*, vol. 7/8 (June 1996), pp. 40–1.

Petat, Jacques, 'L'Ouverteure de *le Maudit*', *Cinéma*, col. 282, June 1982, pp. 55–60.

Ropars-Wuilleumier, Marie-Claire, 'M comme montage', in *Le texte divisé* (Paris: puf, 1981), pp. 93–104.

Schönemann, Heide, *Fritz Lang: Filmbilder, Vorbilder* (Berlin: Edition Hentrich, 1992).

Simsolo, Noel, Bernard Eisenschitz & Gérard Legrand, M le Maudit: *un film de Fritz Lang* (Paris: Calman-Levy, 1990).

Stevens, Dana, 'Writing, Scratching, and Politics from *M* to *Mabuse*', *Qui Parle*, vol. 7 no. 1, Fall/Winter 1993, pp. 57–80.

Sturm, Georges, *Fritz Lang: films, textes, references*. (Nancy: Presses Universitaires de Nancy, 1990).

Tatar, Maria, 'The Killer as Victim: Fritz Lang's *M*', in *Lustmord: Sexual Murder in Weimar Germany* (Princeton: Princeton University Press, 1995), pp. 153–72.

Wagner, Patrick, *Volksgemeinschaft ohne Verbrechen: Konzeptionen und Praxis der Kriminalpolizei in der Zeit der Weimarer Republik und des Nationalsozialismus* (Hamburg: Hans Christians Verlag, 1996).

Woods, Paul Anthony, 'The Silver Screen Shadows of Weimar', in *Monsters of Weimar* (London: Nemesis Books, 1993), pp. 293–396.

ALSO PUBLISHED

If you would like further information about future BFI Film Classics or about other books on film, media and popular culture from BFI Publishing, please write to:

**BFI Film Classics
BFI Publishing
21 Stephen Street
London W1P 2LN**